Praise f
TRA

MW00880183

"Why am I here? Why is there human suffering? Why am I suffering ... and in such a stuck, familiar kind of way? At some point, most of us ask such questions. Many of us start by trying to change outer circumstances. Eventually, though, we realize that lasting change is an inside job. What joy there is in finding effective tools and techniques for inner change! I am so grateful for Diana's work in writing this book in which seekers discover many different tools to try. May each reader be blessed with the courage to build support and community with these tools."
—Pierre Couvillion, School of Ayurveda, Yoga,
Meditation and Bodywork, www.santosha-school.com

"*Traveling Spirit* is a tremendously personal and passionate resource for anyone who desires spiritual growth. No matter what has started one down this path—be it grief, loss, addiction, or the simple a desire to expand one's consciousness—the tools of recovery and growth are beautifully inventoried and demystified within the pages of this book. This book is a sometimes poignant but always joyous reminder that the journey of spirituality and recovery can begin with just one step ... one breath, one thought, or one moment at a time."
—Kim I. Manlove, Co-Chair of the Parent Advisory Board
and Parent Ambassador of THE PARTNERSHIP AT
DRUGFREE.ORG, www.drugfree.org; Founding Board
Member of The 24 Group

"Diana Ensign's *Traveling Spirit* encourages the reader to reach for age-old practices that have endorsed health and happiness throughout time and across cultures. Writing with clarity and a biographical narrative approach, Ensign's book is filled with examples revealing how she has received support and spiritual sustenance in her life. Especially helpful are the questions and discussion points in each chapter. Studied alone or in a small group setting, *Traveling Spirit* is a helpful tool for personal growth and renewal."
—Rev. Amy Kindred, Unitarian Universalist Minister
Unitarian Universalist Fellowship of Charlotte County, Florida

"Diana Ensign's book, *Traveling Spirit*, offers a wonderful and invaluable array of tools for spiritual development, all in one place, as well as practical ways to incorporate a consistent spiritual practice into our hectic daily lives. Diana's sharing of her personal experiences help give meaning and depth to the different spiritual practices leading to our spiritual growth—the most important journey of all."

—Ingrid Mateos, Designer of Conscious MOVEment Meditation. www.consciousdancer.com

TRAVELING SPIRIT

Daily Tools for Your Life's Journey

DIANA J. ENSIGN, JD

BALBOA.
PRESS
A DIVISION OF HAY HOUSE

Copyright © 2013 Diana J. Ensign, JD.

All rights reserved. No part of this book may be used or reproduced by any means, graphic, electronic, or mechanical, including photocopying, recording, taping or by any information storage retrieval system without the written permission of the publisher except in the case of brief quotations embodied in critical articles and reviews.

Book cover photograph by Marg Herder, www.circlewebworks.com
Book cover design by Kate Oberreich, www.kateoberreich.com

Balboa Press books may be ordered through booksellers or by contacting:

Balboa Press
A Division of Hay House
1663 Liberty Drive
Bloomington, IN 47403
www.balboapress.com
1-(877) 407-4847

Because of the dynamic nature of the Internet, any web addresses or links contained in this book may have changed since publication and may no longer be valid. The views expressed in this work are solely those of the author and do not necessarily reflect the views of the publisher, and the publisher hereby disclaims any responsibility for them.

The author of this book does not dispense medical advice or prescribe the use of any technique as a form of treatment for physical, emotional, or medical problems without the advice of a physician, either directly or indirectly. The intent of the author is only to offer information of a general nature to help you in your quest for emotional and spiritual well-being. In the event you use any of the information in this book for yourself, which is your constitutional right, the author and the publisher assume no responsibility for your actions.

ISBN: 978-1-4525-7373-1 (sc)
ISBN: 978-1-4525-7375-5 (hc)
ISBN: 978-1-4525-7374-8 (e)

Library of Congress Control Number: 2013908235

Printed in the United States of America.

Balboa Press rev. date: 06/07/2013

TABLE OF CONTENTS

*To Spirit for bringing Indigo, Emmeline, and Dave
into my life and for helping me to discover moments of joy.
To Trees ... for bringing healing.*

"We are not human beings having a spiritual experience; we are spiritual beings having a human experience."
—Pierre Teilhard de Chardin
(French Jesuit priest)

PREFACE

Beginning a Spiritual Journey

"As I walk, as I walk, the Universe is walking with me"
—from a Navajo rain dance ceremony

A story in American Indian traditions tells of a white buffalo calf woman who brings a Sacred Pipe for the joining of people to Spirit. As told by Bear Heart, in *The Wind Is My Mother*, one Lakota version of the legend is that Sun and Moon have a daughter, Morning Star. Known as "Most Beautiful One," she arrives as a white buffalo calf that turns into a beautiful maiden. Two men see her. One has lust in his heart and quickly disappears, enveloped by Spirit. The other man shows her respect. It is him that she sends to gather people for the teachings of the Sacred Pipe. According to legend, the bowl of the Pipe represents the Universe and the stem Humankind—all connected, one to the other. Wisdom of All Creation is at the center. The smoke carries the people's prayers up to Spirit.

My grandmother's ancestry is of the Ojibway/Anishinabe (Chippewa) tribe of St. Joseph Island, Ontario. Yet, I didn't grow up hearing stories of Spirit. My grandmother never openly discussed her family heritage or her spiritual beliefs. Likely, she learned to deny her Indian roots at a young age while attending school—just as she learned not to use her left hand for writing despite being left-handed (a ruler whipped across her knuckles made that point).

Her first husband, who was not Native American, left her with five children to raise and support. Much later, she married again, this time to a man whose family came to America from Poland; the man I call grandfather. My grandparents found work at the Chrysler automobile plant in Michigan—until a forklift driver accidentally rammed into my grandmother's leg, forcing her to take permanent disability. Growing up, I listened to my grandmother share funny family stories about raising her children. None of her stories discussed her Native American heritage. With her death, those stories have been lost.

I wanted this book, which discusses various spiritual practices and paths to wholeness, to include the American Indian voice. As an adult, Native American ceremonies showed me how to travel with Spirit. They also taught me to view Mother Earth—and all her inhabitants—in a sacred manner. Along the way, I also discovered that my writings are my form of prayer. I ask Spirit to guide me, help me to be of service, and carry the message wherever it needs to go. This book is my offering and my deepest prayer for you as you embark on your own traveling spirit voyage.

~ ~ ~

How do you begin a spiritual quest? In the *Tao Te Ching* it is said, "The journey of a thousand miles begins beneath one's feet." Interestingly, that well-known quote doesn't necessarily mean walking. The journey of the Tao is an inner exploration deeply connected to the source of all. It begins within.

However, most people don't wake up one morning and say: "I think I'll go on a spiritual journey today." If everything in your life is perfect, you probably aren't highly motivated to make changes or explore the inner longings of your heart. It's when things go horribly wrong that we start seeking answers.

That's certainly true for me.

For the first 30 years of my life, I had no religious or spiritual affiliations. My parents married young and, like many families in the 1960s, the Vietnam War played a significant role in our lives. After my father's military service, he and my mother divorced. To avoid paying child support, he returned to Vietnam as a civilian, married a Vietnamese woman, and had a family there. He left when I was 4. I never knew him. My mother then married a man who inspected engines at Detroit Diesel Allisonville, while she worked in school cafeterias and later in school custodial and grounds crew positions. I grew up in Dearborn, a middle-class neighborhood located outside Detroit. Addictions were part and parcel of our family makeup.

When I finished high school, my parents couldn't afford to send me to college. Because my mom worked for the school system, I was able to attend Henry Ford Community College for free. With the help of federal grants, scholarships, loans, personal savings, and work-study program, I later transferred to the University of Michigan in Ann Arbor, where I majored in English. After graduation, I worked a couple of years out East as an editor for a division of Simon and Schuster.

I had read *To Kill a Mocking Bird* and, a few years later, determined that law would be a way for me to put my writing to good use. I got accepted to Wayne State University Law School in Detroit; and, upon graduation, was offered a job at a law firm in Indianapolis that focused on employment discrimination cases. Shortly thereafter, I married someone I had met in Detroit whose interest was in the area of labor history. For most of these years, I simply went through the motions of living out my life.

It wasn't until I became the mother of two daughters that the question of religion even came up. When young, my daughters started asking about God. They wanted to know what religion we were and what I believed. I asked, "What do *you* think about God?" My youngest replied, "I think God could be a watermelon. Or a bunny rabbit." After mulling it over, I said, "Well, that could be true. Nobody knows for certain." We all giggled. But their questions did start the ball rolling.

When a neighbor invited our family to visit a Unitarian Universalist church, it sounded like a suitable place for my children's religious education. A Unitarian Universalist church encourages a free and open search for religious truth. At that time, it hadn't occurred to me that I might need spirituality in my own life.

The first inkling that things in my life were amiss, which I chose to ignore, took place after a weekend work blitz. I was working as an attorney on a class action lawsuit and arrived home after not sleeping for 72 hours. While heading toward the house, I saw my daughter, who was a toddler at the time, waiting on the top porch step. She excitedly started toward me and then toppled forward. I watched her—my brain moving in a slow motion time warp—as she fell toward the sidewalk. I couldn't move. My husband came rushing outside when he heard her wailing. I just stood there, dazed. Fortunately, she wasn't seriously injured. After making my way to bed, I woke up that night with my entire arm numb and thought I was having a stroke. Sometimes we get an obvious wake-up call—a universal two-by-four—telling us that our lives need to change, but we refuse to listen.

Another incident that finally did get my attention took place a few years later. Early one morning, my daughter and I were waiting for her school bus. She had just started kindergarten. My daughter was sitting on an upside down coffee can that she had carried with her to the bus stop. I glanced over. Her fist was clenched tight under her chin and her face scrunched in consternation. I asked her what she was thinking. She said, "I am thinking about how to save the King and Queen."

Earlier that morning, my (now former) husband and I had engaged in a heated argument. I knelt down beside my daughter and said, "Honey, you don't need to worry about daddy and me. That's for grown-ups." She stood up, glared at me, and grabbed her coffee can. "YOU cannot tell me what to think about!" she yelled as she turned and marched off.

Although I recognized that the arguments with my husband were affecting our children, I didn't know what to do. I desperately wanted to avoid repeating negative patterns into the next generation. But I was so caught up in in the whirl of work, fighting, raising children, and exhaustion that I didn't know how to stop the cycle.

Around this same time, I hit a breaking point. My mother telephoned to tell me that my biological father had died in an alcohol-related driving accident. He and a friend were leaving a bar, and their car had a head-on collision with another vehicle. Both my father and his friend were killed. After the Vietnam War, my father had returned to the States with his Vietnamese wife and their children. At the time of his death, he was 55 years old. I hadn't seen him since I was 4.

That telephone call felt like a kick in the gut. All the years of denial—the repressed suffering, loneliness, and heartache—hit home with a vengeance. Despite not having seen him in over 30 years,

I suddenly knew: This man is my father. The knowing wasn't a rational, thinking awareness. I felt it in the molecules swirling around madly inside me. The ache was unbearable.

When the pain and suffering get bad enough, we do the only thing left to do: We ask for help.

Thus began my spiritual journey.

INTRODUCTION

*"If you really want to help this world, what you'll have
to teach is how to live in it."*
—Joseph Campbell

Everyone's life follows a unique spiritual path, depending on what the heart and soul yearn for most. When you are completely open—meaning that you're no longer trying to dictate, control, or hide from life—what you need arrives.

This book offers simple techniques that promote wholeness. Undertaking a path of learning, growing, and healing can be some of the most challenging work you do. You are asked to face your biggest fears, admit your vulnerabilities, and tackle your toughest problems in new ways. You are asked to become honest with yourself! Beginning a spiritual venture requires tremendous courage and resolve. Fortunately, we each have access to resources that make this journey possible. Spiritual tools help us along and provide lifelines when the going gets tough.

When I finally sought help, a family member directed me to Al-Anon, a recovery program for friends and family members of those with alcohol drinking problems. My sister, who works in the field of addictions and recovery, realized I hadn't faced the disease of alcoholism that had so greatly impacted our upbringing. In the Al-Anon program, I was introduced to the notion that a higher power could serve as a source of healing—though I wasn't yet applying this idea to my life. With my father's death, I started asking questions about life and about suffering: *Why do some people make it through adversities in a healthy way and others self-destruct? What might have made a difference in my father's life? What helps alleviate human suffering?* His death—and the intensity of my emotional pain—made answering these questions imperative.

In my need to understand, I began interviewing veterans who had learned useful healing methods to navigate through suffering. I'm lucky that as a writer, I can always gain knowledge by sitting down with someone, asking questions, and taking notes for an article, book, or story. Rather than applying my writing and investigative skills to the law, I directed my efforts toward gathering spiritual information. Many of the veterans I interviewed had undergone a deep soul searching. I listened to their stories. Later, I received an Indiana's artist's grant for a writing project, "Voices of Hope: Veteran Stories of Faith & Healing."

In addition to my father's absence in my life and his unexpected death, my background includes family alcohol and narcotic addictions; a witness to physical and verbal violence; deaths of friends and family members from suicides, overdoses, and substance abuse; a miscarriage; a divorce; single parenting; and loss of my job during the economic recession. While difficult and, at times, emotionally devastating, these life experiences did not defeat me. On the contrary, they taught me important life lessons and led my life in new, positive directions. I would never wish suffering on anyone. Yet, such intense suffering can also carry with it unexpected gifts.

My experiences made me committed to spending quality time with my children and showing them unconditional love, to finding positive solutions to age-old problems, and to working hard at understanding the disease of addiction. I have dedicated my life to seeking healthy, spiritual methods for alleviating human suffering.

After my father's death, I started meditating. I also attended a Wisdom Circle with a group of women friends. Wisdom Circles are small group listening circles based on Native American, Twelve Step, and Quaker principles. Years later, I learned meditative practices such as T'ai Chi and Qigong. I walked labyrinths, practiced yoga, drummed, danced, and continually stayed open for guidance. That guidance frequently came in unexpected forms. I was invited to a Buddhist meditation sangha, Goddess rituals, American Indian ceremonies, a Vision Quest, and shaman workshops. I received Master Certification in Reiki energy healing, and I read the *Upanishads*, *Tao Te Ching*, and numerous spiritual books from a variety of faith traditions. Strangely, the prompting to read the *Upanishads* came to me in a dream. Additional spiritual teachings arrived from nature, my children, and a wide circle of friends.

I now firmly believe that a life of Spirit makes a qualitative difference in people's daily lives and in their potential for true happiness. Following a spiritual path may not be the only answer for our individual and collective problems. But it's certainly one that helped me and unquestionably aided countless others. Throughout the ages and across the globe, world renowned leaders have advocated for just such a life—including spiritual teachers such as Siddhartha (the Buddha), Gandhi, Jesus, Dr. Martin Luther King Jr., Peace Pilgrim, Bear Heart, Mother Teresa, Muhammad, Nelson Mandela, the Dalai Lama, Wilma Mankiller, Thich Nhat Hanh, Starhawk, and so on. Whether you refer to your spiritual source as Creator, Spirit, God, Universal Energy, Great Mystery, Conscious Awareness,

Higher Power, the Feminine Divine, Goddess, Love, the Tao, or by some other name ... it doesn't matter!

What matters is having that Source accessible when you need it and applying it to your life in practical and usable ways.

~ ~ ~

I invite you to begin your journey toward wholeness and healing. Ask Spirit to guide you. Ask loved ones to support you. "Give thanks for unknown blessings already on their way," according to a Native American saying. Or as my daughters like to say before meals: **"I have gratitude for the whole wide world and everything in between."**

Let's begin, together.

In joy & gratitude,

—Diana J. Ensign, JD

CHAPTER 1

BREATH: Your Greatest Resource

"There is only one journey. Going inside yourself."
—Rainer Maria Rilke

Each Sunday, a meditation group I attend gathers at a nearby Japanese-style home. During my walking meditations through the flower gardens and along the creek, I always notice a wooden sign posted on the other side of the creek's bank. It reads simply: **Breathe.**

Over and over again in meditation books and teachings, students are instructed to pay attention to their breath. It may sound easy when someone says, "Remember to breathe." But try it the next time you feel angry or heartbroken. Notice how hard it is to simply pause and take three deep breaths. Of course, for most healthy people it's not physically difficult to take three deep breaths. However, it is emotionally difficult. Your hurt or angry emotions want to jump in and take charge. Unfortunately, like a bad TV reality show, your emotions can get you caught up in high drama—with terrible and sometimes life-threatening consequences. Pausing to focus on your breath requires extreme effort in the heat of the moment. With practice, though, breath awareness can become a useful new habit. Try it now. **Take three deep breaths ....**

On a spiritual journey, your breath is your most effective tool—soothing mind, body, and spirit. Breath links you to the universal life force energy. This life force energy is referred to as chi, qi, ki, prana, mana, and various other names throughout the world. Some people view it as white light or healing light. Others visualize it as blue energy or swirling, star-filled space containing all the galaxies. In Native American traditions, when you empty out hate, anger, fear, and resentment—becoming like hollow bones—the breath of Spirit moves through you. Imagine this: Your breath has the ability to directly connect you to God—or whatever word you use to signify the Source of all.

Before heading into the chaos or crisis of your day, take a few deep breaths. If your day begins with a crying child, a blaring alarm clock, hectic rush-hour traffic, or an emergency wake-up call, allow 10 seconds to just breathe. Take a few intentional breaths en route if necessary—as you walk, as you drive, or while in the bathroom. When facing a troubling situation, remind yourself: **"Yesterday is gone. Tomorrow has not yet happened."** You are simply in this moment. Whether this moment is good, bad, or neutral, it will pass. As my mother often jokes when asked how she's doing: "I didn't see my name in the obituaries today; so far, so good."

Take a few breaths now before proceeding further. Set a pause alarm in your mind that says *breathe* as you begin each chapter. With this one tool, you'll notice a huge improvement in your life. It may not seem all that important, but the next time you're confronted with a life challenge, you'll be glad that you learned how to slow down and pay attention to your breath.

Practice, Practice, Practice

A friend who works with the disease of addiction explained to me that breath awareness is the one tool he always recommends to those in recovery because it breaks the cycle of impulse behavior. Breath allows a pause. In that pause, you can keep your composure and maintain your emotional balance when all else is falling apart.

When you feel your emotions making that familiar roller coaster climb, take a deep breath before racing full speed ahead. During that brief pause, feel the emotions in your body. Is there tightness in your chest, a shortness of breath, a tension headache, or a racing heartbeat? Use your body to remind you: **Keep breathing**. When you slow down to breathe, you'll gain some control over your thoughts, emotions, and behavior. You don't have to follow a path that's destructive to your wellness. Practice your breathing the next time your emotions start to skyrocket. Note: It will be easier if you practice before they escalate. Don't worry if it doesn't go well at first. You'll likely get plenty of opportunity for practice. We all do. My counselor likes to suggest a large supply of "do-overs."

Using breath as a tool is helpful whether you're relating to an irritable child, a disgruntled teen, a disagreeable boss, a contentious relative, a difficult co-worker, a hostile ex-spouse, an angry romantic partner, a verbally abusive parent, or an unfriendly neighbor. In Buddhism, such people are referred to as your teachers. The lesson is this: **You can't change other people; but you can learn to breathe.**

Whenever I sense conflict, fear, or anxiety rising in myself or someone else, I breathe deeply so that I can better assess the situation. That momentary pause may not always stop such emotions. However, it can prevent a bad situation from escalating. One time, my boss sent me an email with instructions to come to his office NOW. He had a reputation for angry outbursts, so I took a few deep breaths and walked to the restroom. I got a drink of water and then I walked slowly to his office, breathing mindfully with each step. As I listened to him, I realized he was upset about my work schedule (even though we had discussed it, and he had approved it). I quietly explained that I was following the schedule on which we had agreed. Despite feeling nervous, my breathing allowed me to speak clearly and calmly. There was nothing else to say or argue. Eventually, he calmed down and assured me that he wasn't going to fire me.

Even if the other person stays furious, calming your emotions—rather than merely reacting to situations—gives you an opportunity to figure out the next right thing to say or do. With my boss, getting fired was not in my best interest at that time. Months later, when he did fire me, I was more prepared to leave that antagonistic work environment. I never felt a need to argue. His anger had nothing to do with me.

Another time, I had pulled into a gas station to fill up my car's gas tank. While I was pumping the gas, a man across the way started screaming and calling out angrily, "Infidel! You are an infidel!" Busy watching the pump, I was thinking, *I wonder who he's yelling at? Infidel isn't a common word people shout at each other.* As the man gradually wandered off, still yelling and mumbling, he was pointing a finger in my direction.

As I was putting on the gas cap, I suddenly realized that he had been pointing at my bumper sticker, which reads, "Coexist" and contains various religious symbols. Because it hadn't occurred to me that his yelling was aimed at me, I didn't feel angry or scared. I felt reasonably neutral. Afterward, I wondered if it would be possible to feel that calm knowing full well that someone was deliberately directing his or her negativity in my direction. I realized that if I had known that man was angrily calling me an infidel, nothing in the situation would have changed—only my reaction to it.

Remember, another person's anger may have more to do with that person's stress and anxieties than with anything you did or didn't do. You'll often witness examples of this kind of anger in traffic jams or in long lines where people start to feel impatient. In these situations, allowing a few moments to just breathe can help calm your mental state. As Eleanor Roosevelt said, "No one can make you feel inferior without your consent." **Likewise, someone else's anger does not need to ruin your day.**

Breathing Tip

The next time you feel your emotions churning, stop whatever you're doing and take three breaths. Focusing on your breath will get you out of chaotic thinking. If you can't remember to count your breaths, create a trigger word or action that reminds you to pause. Drink a cup of tea, take a walk, say a silent prayer, or take a time out.

I don't want to imply that this breathing practice is easy. Breathing and working through strong emotions such as anger or fear are extremely tough things to do. It's easier to blame someone, slam a door, drive off in a fit of anger, and plot revenge. Anger, revenge, and hatred don't require much effort. But such knee-jerk responses don't solve your problems, and they don't solve the world's problems. Resolving conflicts and facing your emotions requires inner resolve rather than the physical strength of "might makes right." Peacemakers such as Gandhi, Jesus, and Dr. King recognized that inner peace is necessary to create peace in the world. As noted in the quote in the introduction of this book, "**As you walk, the Universe is walking with you.**"

The good news is that you can use your breath as a tool wherever you go, and you can practice using it daily. During intense conflict, you might find yourself forgetting to take a few deep breaths. Don't worry. Practice breath awareness. Focus on the times when you did remember to breathe. **Then next time, practice again.**

Practice Pointers: "BREATHE"

- **Write "breathe" on a 3 x 5 card.**
- **Post it on your refrigerator, bathroom mirror, or office corkboard.**
- **Put it in your monthly calendar reminders.**
- **Keep the breathe notecard in your wallet, notebook, or coat pocket.**
- **Write "breathe" in your daily journal.**
- **Adopt a trigger word or action that helps you pause.**
- **Create a breathing space. Light a candle or ask for a hug.**

Stress Management

Stress can contribute to various physical ailments. If you want to lower your stress levels, start by working with your breath. We get so embroiled in projects, plans, dramas, anger, and deadlines that we don't notice our breathing. You'll be amazed how beneficial deep breathing is for dealing with daily annoyances and frustrations.

In serious situations (such as an illness, loss of a loved one, severe conflict, or high-pressure situation) deep breathing, along with outside assistance, can help you better manage such times of crisis.

Early in my first marriage, when I was working full time and had young children, every Christmas holiday I became ill. I was trying to please relatives who lived out of state and wanted to see their grandchildren; I was trying to please the people I worked for by getting all my work done; I was trying to please my young children by shopping for wonderful Christmas gifts from Santa; and I was trying to please visitors and family members with a clean house and good meals. But, I was making myself physically sick in the process.

When your body is stressed, your immune system is weakened and can't as easily fight off colds or other illnesses. It's similar to plants during a drought; they become physically weakened. Making time in your life to focus on your breath allows your body to relax. Relaxation helps you pay attention to your health and avoid the frenetic behavior that can contribute to sickness.

Sometimes, when I get into disagreements with a family member, I take a relaxing bath or hot shower. The bath or shower isn't intended as avoidance or as an opportunity to rally my arguments. Rather, it's a soothing period so I can slow down enough to gain some perspective on the situation. That pause enables me to ask myself whether the dispute is worth all the drama and emotion I've attached to it. On a scale of 1 to 10, should it be a two rather than an eight? Is someone just having a bad day? Am I just feeling tired and crabby? **As they say in recovery programs, "How important is it?"**

Notice how you breathe when experiencing stress. When restricted, a lack of breath causes physical pain. A few years ago, I started exercising at the gym with my daughters. As I jogged around the indoor track, I got intense side cramps and quickly became short of breath. Not in the habit of running, I didn't know how to pace myself. I hadn't learned that short rapid breaths would soon tire me. Slowing my pace and calming my breathing avoided the intense cramps. I realized I could apply that lesson to my spiritual practice. In tense circumstances, I can pause, notice my breath, and slow my mental, emotional, and physical pace.

The gift of breath awareness is a calm inner state that leads to a calm outer state. When calm, you can think and act in a manner that serves your highest good. **In any stressful or challenging situation, remember to breathe.**

Breath as Your Teacher

Discover what your breath has to teach you. Even with deep breathing, we get emotionally charged. Emotions can show what is important in your relationships, where you need to set boundaries, and what is unacceptable behavior in the workplace or in the family. Attention to your breath gives you a chance to discern what you need, rather than expending energy trying to change or control someone else.

Breath awareness also provides a space for wisdom to emerge. In our personal interactions, it's not always obvious when someone is suffering. One of my co-workers fit the stereotype of a tough older Italian male, much like a Robert De Niro film character. He used no-nonsense, street-smart language and had a harsh demeanor. He was married with grown children, and he was a grandfather. We were all surprised when he killed himself. It was unexpected and didn't match my image of what someone who commits suicide looks like. In fact, he had joked with me about suicide, and I never realized he was serious.

It's said that you can't judge a book by its cover. The same is true of the people we meet. We don't know what wounds they carry, what hardships they endure, or what struggles they face. Sorrow does not discriminate. It doesn't care about your race, class, intelligence, social standing, looks, popularity, or possessions. When someone we love dies, when we face a terminal illness, or when our lives are in crisis, what remains is our humanity and spirit. The woman behind the counter may have lost her son; the man changing your tire may be in the midst of a divorce; and the clerk at the store may have a relative in the intensive care unit at the hospital. If you are quick to fly off the handle and angrily berate people, you may be doing more harm than you intend.

While in high school, I was on the cheerleading squad, had blond hair, and got decent grades. Yet, inside, I was desperately struggling to make it through each day. One Saturday afternoon, I was sitting on my bedroom floor sorting clothes. Alone in the house, I thought I heard an intruder, which turned out to be a noise next door. But for those few minutes, I had felt very scared. Afterward, I realized that I would be frightened if someone actually broke in and tried to kill me. That realization helped me understand that I didn't really want to die or kill myself; I was just in enormous emotional pain. At that age, I didn't know how to articulate my suffering. So instead, I went numb. For years, if you had asked how I felt, I would have looked at you blankly. I felt nothing.

Two other students in my high school were not as fortunate: one hung himself, and the other we believe shot himself. It's important to note that it's not always clear which teenage deaths are accidental and which are intentional. Having been in that internal state of suffering, I feel enormous empathy for young people. I remember how confusing that time period can be when the adults and world around you don't seem to make sense. For teens, I want to tell you: Life does get better. Don't give up! Seek outside help. For parents, I want to say: Have patience with all that you do not understand.

When irritated, breathe. When angry, breathe. Practice deep breathing in any situation requiring emotional calm and mental clarity. If you're going through extreme personal struggles, breathe. Sometimes, that's the best we can do. Sometimes, that's all that is asked of us.

A Path to Sanity

We hurt ourselves when we surrender our peace of mind. It's often said that being angry with someone is like drinking poison and expecting the other person to get sick … or like carrying around a hot coal. A co-worker used to remind me whenever I complained about my former husband: **"Don't let other people take up space in your mind rent-free."** Focus on your breath and shift your attention. Whenever you feel your body tense because of bad news, conflict, anger, stress, or fear, take a deep breath … then let it out. As you grow calmer, you learn to internally relax. You learn to let go. **You learn … to breathe … at a rhythm … that slows you down.**

In my current marriage, my husband and I are continually working to gain better skills for healthy conflict resolution. We try not to focus our disagreements on "right and wrong." Rather, we communicate feelings and needs and listen to the other person express his or her feelings and needs. What I've learned is that it's absolutely crucial to speak from the heart and not just from the intellect. None of that is possible during a storm of powerful emotions. That's when taking a few deep breaths comes in handy.

Breathing helps you reconnect with your heart. What initially felt like anger may require a deeper look at an old wound. Breathing allows compassion, healing, and love to surface. When my husband and I breathe and speak from the heart, we gain a better understanding of each other and of ourselves. By remaining calm, our rational thinking and problem-solving skills can emerge. Breathing produces a calmer emotional and mental state.

Your breath allows you to ride out the tidal wave of emotions. During one of my daughter's birthday party sleepovers, her kitten died. I was astonished as I watched how each young child processed this sad news: one child was angry, one child was crying, and one child was quietly consoling the child who was crying. We gathered together in a circle, and each girl expressed her feelings. We planned a burial for the kitten (which was one of the girl's ideas). After about 45 minutes, the young girls all ran off to the playground. Children don't attach extra baggage to an event. They stay in the present moment. They feel what they feel, without hiding their emotions or judging them. Then they feel something different.

In the midst of upheavals, find a way to calm your breathing. In Buddhism, the chime of the bell or harmonics of a singing bowl act as a reminder to pause, pay attention, stop for a moment, and just breathe. Other religions use daily prayer at regular intervals as a reminder: **Pause, breathe, reflect, ask for guidance, and give thanks.**

Breathing Tip

Discover your own methods for improving your breath awareness. Put these breath reminders to use while eating, as you walk to the restroom, before getting out of bed, or before going to sleep. At your workplace, the grocery store, a family meeting or funeral, take a few deep breaths. Observe the times where you remembered to take a few slow breaths. Notice the effect it has on your well-being.

About six years ago, I attended a funeral service for the son of friends. The young man who died was in college, and his car overturned when navigating a curve (I talk about his dad's healing process more in the upcoming Reiki section in Chapter 3). While this couple greeted the many visitors who came to mourn his loss, I sat down a few rows back from where they stood. I focused all my attention on calm deep breathing. The dad came up to me afterward and thanked me for "breathing for him." I never told him what I was doing, and I'm not sure how it helped. Yet, those calm deep breaths did somehow get sent his way.

I don't have the answers as to why we're here or what it all means. I do know, however, that tools such as breath awareness help me appreciate the journey and continue on after a fall. If you practice breath awareness during calm periods, it will be available to you in situations where you really need it. When we pause and breathe, we ask questions that matter, and we find the answers we need. **Start with your breath.**

Exercise: Work With Your Breath for Three Weeks

Make a decision to work with your breath for three weeks. Pay attention to your breathing when you're upset. Observe your breathing while driving. Become aware of your breathing before you begin a challenging task. Take a momentary pause before cooking dinner. Pause and breathe before each meal. Pause and breathe before speaking to someone about something important. Keep a journal to track your progress. See if your life changes as you learn to ... pause ... and breathe.

CHAPTER 2

MIND: Using Thoughts Wisely

"Develop such mental power that you can stand unshaken,
no matter what comes, bravely facing anything in life."
—Paramahansa Yogananda (Indian yogi, 1893-1952)

Your mind is a powerful tool on your spiritual journey. Thoughts affect your mood, perspective of events, and perception of others. Research indicates that you have approximately 60,000 thoughts per day—90 percent of which are repetitive! Imagine the incredible improvements you can make in your life simply by changing your thoughts. Religious leader Ernest Holmes, author of *The Science of Mind*, based his spiritual philosophy on this principle.

Learning to direct your thoughts takes practice. There's a popular Buddhist story of a monkey that reaches into a jar with a narrow opening to get the banana inside. When the hunters arrive, the monkey can't get its hand out of the jar opening because it is tightly clenching the banana. This story (while perhaps offensive to those who love animals) is meant to illustrate how we cling to our thoughts, tightly and often futilely. The drama, storyline, and mental churning become the banana in the jar. If you re-create conversations, judgments, opinions, worries, and internal turmoil long after an event has passed, you are clinging to the banana.

The solution in the story, and life, is simple: Let go! But as most of us know, that's not easy in the midst of conflict. Even for practicing Buddhists, who are familiar with the above story, letting go of turbulent thoughts is often a challenge. Once while trick-or-treating with my daughters, I heard two parents arguing as they walked with their young child. Obviously divorced or separated, they were loudly disputing who would spend time with the child during Christmas. They lost their current Halloween with this child over a future holiday. Interestingly, the child's Halloween costume was a striped prison uniform.

I've argued enough with my former husband about the children's visitation, holiday schedules, and expenses to know how emotional those topics can get. I also recognize my tendency to mull over hurts and resentments long after a dispute has ended. **Of course, when parents refuse to release conflicts, it's the children who suffer.**

In truth, we cause ourselves much unnecessary suffering! For years, relatives and friends told me I worried too much. I always rejected such comments with, "Of course, I worry. I'm a mother!" I thought the people giving me advice didn't understand anything about parenting. One day, someone again mentioned my tendency to worry. I suddenly realized I did worry way too much. I wasn't just worrying about an actual event that called for immediate concern; I was worrying about what might happen or what didn't happen or what had previously happened. My worry wasn't just in parenting but in all areas of my life—including my job, relationships, church community, and world events. The problem with all that worry is that it not only eats away at present moments of happiness, it also leads to future problems. For instance, if you're frequently worried that your children won't turn out well, and you constantly berate them to do better or grill them on their faults, you may perpetuate the very thing you're trying to prevent. Your worry is not planting positive seeds in their minds, and it's not helping your peace of mind.

There's a Chinese proverb that says you can't control the birds of worry that fly over your head, but you can prevent them from building a nest in your hair. Most of my imagined worries never happened and, in the meantime, I lost precious time that I could have been enjoying. Even with events that did warrant my real concern, worry didn't solve the problems or help me seek potential solutions. It was just a mental loop I got trapped in.

Fortunately, there are tools to assist with excessive mental churning and "banana clinging." With practice, you can put your mind to better use. As they say in recovery programs, "Do you want to be right, or do you want to be happy?" For divorced parents, I would add: "Do you want to be right, or do you want your children to be happy?" **You have the power to decide.**

Meditation

Meditation is an excellent means for gaining mental clarity. It helps calm the mind so that you can become more aware of repetitive thought patterns. Practicing meditation doesn't necessarily stop mental chatter. It also doesn't require or produce complete mental silence. Meditation means you stop talking and focus on your breath. As you do so, you begin to notice your incessant thinking and your internal worrying, judging, arguing, and analyzing. Once you see your patterns, you can work on changing them or accepting them without blame, guilt, or judgment. Like watching clouds pass overhead, meditation allows you to observe thoughts, emotions, and body sensations. With self-observation comes greater insight, and with greater insight comes wisdom.

The intent of meditation is to bring awareness and mindfulness to the present moment. You can then apply that mindfulness to every aspect of your life.

How Do You Start a Meditation Practice?

To begin, find a comfortable position. Your meditation can last for whatever time allotment you want or no particular amount of time. You can sit anywhere you can relax—a pillow, chair, couch, or bed. You can sit under a tree, at your desk at work during a break, or in your car in a parking lot.

During the sitting meditation, one approach is to count each breath in and each breath out until your reach 10. Then begin again. Another meditation method might be to focus on a mantra, phrase, or chant. Some people bring in light or surround their body in light. Some listen to meditative tapes. Others drum.

A common meditation practice is to pay attention to how your body feels. Is your body tense? Is it relaxed? If your body is tense, internally relax your breathing. When your breathing is steady, focus on where you feel tension in your body. Then become aware of an area, such as your toes or fingertips, where you don't feel tension. Switching your focus back and forth between the two areas can help you relax the tense parts of your body. If your body is tense because of physical discomfort, try another position. Your meditation practice shouldn't produce physical pain.

While meditating, be aware of your thoughts as they pass, but don't get too caught in the storylines. Try not to worry about whether you're doing the meditation correctly. You don't need a specific objective or goal. Just breathe. Over time, you'll gain awareness of when your mind is scattered and when you're present, here and now. You may experience states of peace, grief, love, anger, or confusion. The moments pass. Whatever shows up, sit with it. Let the emotions flow through your body and mind. **Keep meditating.**

The Following are Meditation Methods You Can Try:

Sitting Meditation

My initial approach to meditation was to check out a library book on meditation. After reading the book, I began meditating at night while sitting in bed. I meditated for about 20 minutes right before sleep.

One Friday evening, I decided to attend a Greek play, *Lysistrata*. I saw a woman I recognized with a group of people, and she asked me to join them. It turned out that the people in the group all attended the same Buddhist meditation sangha. After chatting for a while, they invited me to visit a Sunday gathering. I had never heard the word sangha, but they were friendly. So I agreed.

A sangha, it turns out, is a community of people who regularly meet to strengthen and support their sitting meditation practice. At first, I felt trepidation. I was unfamiliar with Buddhism and with the meditation practices of a sangha. I worried that maybe the group was a cult, or maybe the gathering was a way to get money from people.

These gentle people met in a Japanese-style home with a beautifully tended garden. The group sat in silent meditation for

20 minutes, walked silently outdoors for 20 minutes, drank tea silently for 20 minutes, and then held a brief discussion on a book by a Vietnamese Buddhist monk named Thich Nhat Hanh (sangha teachings or discussions are referred to as dharma talks).

Fears of the unknown can be outrageous. Our minds are good at making up stories without any real basis in fact—especially if we grow up hearing horrible news of other countries and religions and don't hear news of the wonderful things those people are doing in the world. After having attended this sangha now for close to a decade, I understand that these individuals are not only committed to their meditation practice, but they are also strongly committed to nonviolence and community outreach. The sangha does not collect money unless the group decides to support a community outreach effort, such as sending items to Haitian schoolchildren. The sangha taught me respectful ways to communicate and respectful ways to walk upon Mother Earth. It taught me not to turn away from my suffering or the suffering of others. I found living models for how I would like to be in the world. My sangha meditation practice continues to be a vital part of my spiritual growth.

Nature Meditation

Nature provides a peaceful environment for meditation. In the early evenings, I take meditative walks to the river and watch what arrives: herons, minks, woodpeckers, ducks, and dragonflies. Once, a heron flew close overhead and landed in the tree across the river. I watched it perched there; I wanted to learn how to land somewhere and just be—without carrying so much fear.

We can learn by observing birds, animals, rivers and streams, trees, insects, and plants. A favorite quote of mine from the classic

Chinese text the *Tao Te Ching* is: **"Man is not the only keeper of enlightenment."** Life is awe-inspiring when we discover how to be like the heron. If we observed where and how animals lived, we wouldn't have yards covered with grass. Grass is a wasteland for animals, especially in winter. They need the tall native prairie grasses, trees, flower stalks, and shrubs for shelter. They need the fruits, vegetation, berries, and, for many insects, pollen. Grass treated by chemical poisons is a deathbed. Ask nature what she has to teach you.

When walking meditatively in natural settings, pay attention. How do you feel walking on leaves or dirt? How do you feel leaning against a tree trunk, sitting on a log, or watching a flowing stream? Stay aware of the present moment. Be mindful of each step, breath, breeze, and sound. Bring your full attention to the fact that you are walking. Behold the sky, birds, tree limbs, and small creatures sharing the space with you. Mother Earth offers spectacular landscapes and quiet vistas for reflective meditation. Likewise with a sitting meditation in nature, breathe and stay connected to your natural environment.

Nature is soothing. Time in nature can mend our sorrows, fears, and loneliness. Relaxing in sunlight and fresh air may also improve your mood, blood pressure, heart rate, and other physical systems. Research indicates that a primary source of Vitamin D is exposure to the sun, and healthy doses of 10 to 15 minutes a day may help with seasonal affective disorder and possibly cancer prevention. Other studies show that wounds heal faster in fresh air.

Early in my first marriage, when my daughter was just over a year old, I became pregnant again. This second pregnancy resulted in a miscarriage during the first trimester. I felt devastated and thought no one understood my suffering. In times of loss and sorrow, people often say things in attempts to help; they mean well. But sometimes words sound cruel to a person who is feeling intensely sad. People inferred that the baby was malformed and that the miscarriage was nature's way of ridding my body of it, or that I was lucky that it happened so early in the pregnancy. During this time, I walked daily to a neighborhood park and sat on a hill near the pine trees. I would lie on my back and ask the tree roots to hold my pain. Nature didn't ask questions of me or give advice or tell me what I "should" do. The trees and sunlight brought only healing. If I had to describe my deepest religious beliefs in one word, I would answer: Trees. I love trees. They seem to hold wisdom far beyond human comprehension.

Years later, when I accepted a job in the city, I used my lunch break to walk to the nearest park and do the same thing: I would find a grassy spot near a tree, lie down, and ask the Earth to hold my stress. If you use a wheelchair or have other walking limitations, look for a park with a wheelchair accessible path. Or try positioning yourself near a tree or see if someone can help you recline beneath a tree. Ask Mother Earth to hold your suffering. **Release your pain, worries, and frustrations to the soil, tree roots, or sun.**

Even if you don't have a nearby a park, a small space with a bird feeder, plants, and sunlight can serve as a meditative setting. Of course, providing more green space in our overcrowded and polluted cities aids not only our health and healing but also provides habitat for many creatures. If your access to natural space is limited, try bringing nature indoors through pictures, plants, or sounds.

Awareness of the natural world expands both mind and heart. Immediate problems don't feel quite so big within the larger landscape of sky, meadows, birds, and trees. Nature connects you to something more than your current struggles. Rather than viewing life as full of stress, worry, and complicated battles, **nature teaches you to view your part in the greater whole and to seek out harmony.**

Labyrinth Meditations

Meditating in a labyrinth can help you work through difficulties. A labyrinth isn't a maze; a maze offers pathway choices and leads to dead ends. A labyrinth is circular. **You don't get lost in a labyrinth; you just travel the path to the center and back out again.** It's an ancient spiral design with the earliest Cretan-style labyrinths dating back 3,500 years. There's also a Chartres-style labyrinth, a more complex circular design based on the permanent stone labyrinth set into the floor of the Chartres Cathedral in France in the 13th century. A beautiful Chartres-style labyrinth can be found in New Harmony, Indiana.

A labyrinth offers several uses. You can walk a labyrinth alone or in a group. You can pose a question, raise a problem, request guidance, or maintain an open mind to whatever comes. You can sing, dance, chant, or walk in silence. You can light candles and take moonlit walks. Labyrinth patterns are often drawn on fabric for indoor use. For outdoor use, labyrinths patterns can be created using stones, bricks, sticks, flowers, candles, or shrubs. Some labyrinths are wheelchair- and walker-accessible. Other labyrinths are handheld, miniature designs in wood or metal that let you trace the path using a pointer.

When encountering trials, using a labyrinth offers a way to slow down and approach the problem from a spiritual dimension. While in the center, you can ask for guidance or strength and release the problem as you walk out. Some people carry an object, such as a stone, to leave in the center. An answer may come immediately, or it may come later. Often, the answer is far less complicated than the issue. A labyrinth allows for a deeper knowing to emerge. For instance, my surface mind may mull over a difficulty with a relationship or a job. While walking the labyrinth, I might realize I need to "trust the universe" or "let it go." Such inner guidance may not arise automatically for most of us because we get caught up in personalities and egos. I don't always know what is best for me or anyone else. In fact, I usually discover that I'm grateful things didn't go the way I thought they should. It's so easy to become mentally preoccupied with what we perceive to be right or wrong. Tools, such as a labyrinth, permit a quiet, reflective space so we can become more aware of helpful insights.

One time while attending a women's weekend drumming retreat, we created a labyrinth and participated in a late night labyrinth walk. The retreat took place about an hour from Indianapolis on a 250-acre site with meadows, trails, woodlands, and organically farmed fields. At the retreat, we learned how to drum, attended workshops on spiritual growth, danced, and shared meals. On the last night, we constructed an outdoor labyrinth with paths illuminated by rows of flickering candles. Some women softly drummed while others practiced meditative movements, such as T'ai Chi, beneath the night stars. I stood at the labyrinth entrance and smudged each woman with the cleansing smoke from a small bundle of burning sage before she walked the ancient spiral. As a result, I was one of the last people to walk the labyrinth. When everyone else had finished, I walked slowly to the center, gazed up at the vast starlit sky and then walked slowly out. After leaving the labyrinth, I rested flat on my back in the grass under the night sky. I felt the Earth shift. The experience filled me with such awe and well-being that I wanted everyone to feel it.

Later, when I returned home, I worked with my church community to build a permanent outdoor labyrinth on our grounds. Since then, the labyrinth we constructed with bricks and small stones has been used for funeral services, peace walks, solstice/equinox celebrations, wisdom circles, and individual walks of sorrow, joy, and healing.

During my divorce, I walked the church labyrinth that I had helped build. At that time, I needed a place to live and had been looking at various homes, feeling overwhelmed by all the decisions I faced. I decided to walk the labyrinth with my daughters. When we reached the center, I intended to drop the small stone I was carrying and ask for guidance on which house would be best for us. When we got to the center, I knew the house I would purchase. I used my rational thinking to narrow the choices, and I used my intuitive and heart choice to make the final decision. The labyrinth assisted me in the process. It was a way to ask Spirit and my heart—not just my head—what was most needed in that situation.

Another time, on a solo retreat in Southern Indiana, I happened upon an outdoor labyrinth partially hidden by tall grass. As I was walking the labyrinth, I saw a fawn sleeping in one of the paths. The young deer looked so beautiful and peaceful. I watched for a moment and then tiptoed away, leaving the labyrinth. The fawn reminded me of my daughters. It reminded me how young children are already on the path, naturally, and we can appreciate where they are, protect their space, and learn from them. It reminded me of my own vulnerability and innocence. It reminded me of that part of myself that wants to feel trust, love, and safety. The sleeping fawn was like a soft whisper carried on the wind: **"Rest peacefully. It will all be OK."**

With labyrinths, you don't focus on an end destination; you just follow the path. A labyrinth can teach that Spirit will see you through. When making a tough decision, if your heart feels tight, like a closed fist, you may need to look more closely at your intentions. A labyrinth can get you in touch with your true feelings and highest desires for your life. If the decision feels right in your heart, from a place of wholeness, you will know it on a deeper level.

An outdoor labyrinth also acts as a reminder that we live upon the Earth and depend upon Mother Earth for our survival. With grocery stores, gas heaters, electric lights, and air conditioners, it's easy to forget that the real source of our survival is Mother Earth. We need the sky, trees, plants, rain, animals, and sun. It's important not to lose our real connection to food, water, air, and heat sources. And we must remember to say thank you for all we receive. With the paper form of this book, I acknowledge the sacrifice of the trees. (See nonprofit Haiti reforestation fund noted in the back section of this book). My awareness of trees used for paper products prompts me to ask whether what I write will make a difference. Walking an outdoor labyrinth reminds me to give thanks to nature. Nature asks that I replenish the lives of the trees I have taken. **When you travel a spiritual path, each step matters. That is a lesson of the labyrinth.**

Daily Meditations

Meditation isn't limited to sitting or walking. Almost any task can be meditative if you stay mindful and focus on your breath. Try meditation while cleaning, working, or tending the garden. Learn to bring your mindfulness into all aspects of your life. The key is to quiet your mind enough to be aware of what you are doing in the moment: washing dishes, folding clothes, cooking dinner, or speaking to someone. Pay attention to the task at hand and not what happened in the past or what might happen in the future. The present moment requires your full and complete awareness. For example, while sitting at the table writing this page, that is all I am doing. Remember, new habits take time. Noticing our emotions, thoughts, and actions requires practice. But doing so provides insight into how much time and energy we put toward past and future conflict, stress, and worry. **We can choose where to focus our attention.**

With a meditation practice, we still face what comes each day. Some days feel joyful and exciting. Other days feel like we're mired in quicksand. Some days show us death, sorrow, conflict, and disappointment. Some days show us the birth of a child and warm spring sunshine. Life continually presents challenges along with pleasant surprises. In each fleeting moment, we decide how we'll respond. My hairdresser's quote on his chalkboard aptly sums up the unpredictability of each new day: **"Life is all about how you handle Plan B."** Meditation helps you be in the moment—whatever that moment brings. Experiment with different meditation methods to discover what works best in your life.

Meditation Pointers:
- **Make your meditation practice a priority in your life.**
- **Spend contemplative time in nature.**
- **Walk a labyrinth.**
- **Practice some form of meditation daily.**

Additional Methods You Can Try:

- **Play meditative music or listen to meditation CDs.**
- **Use a singing bowl to start and end your meditation session. A Tibetan singing bowl is a brass bowl that uses a wooden striker to produce a hum when circling the rim. Keep the singing bowl and a pillow in a visible place.**

Benefits of Meditation

You may not notice immediate benefits to your meditation practice. You might even find the practice disturbing as you become aware of the near impossibility of calming your mind. That doesn't mean the meditation isn't working. On the contrary, becoming conscious of our mental states is a significant achievement. Don't give up because the benefits aren't what you imagined. When someone learns to draw or paint, for example, they first have to learn how to properly use a pencil or paintbrush and paints. That person may then take art classes and sketch or paint for years—producing many beautiful works over time. With practice, you'll uncover the benefits of meditation as well. **But even five minutes of meditation a day over a period of months can greatly improve the quality of your life.**

Inner Calm

Meditation can help ease anxiety. You can use this tool while waiting for someone who is late, while stuck in traffic, or while sitting in a hospital waiting room or airport terminal. After my divorce, I found myself with two children to support. I returned to work after an eight-year hiatus. My busy job in a downtown office building felt overwhelming. Sometimes in the morning, I would sit in my car and sob. At the office, I felt like a butterfly pressed up against a glass pane. I wasn't sure I would survive. When I arrived home in the evening, I meditated for an entire hour just to gain a sense of calm. I kept a pillow on my living room floor to remind me to meditate.

I decided to meditate on my lunch breaks and whenever I needed five minutes to just breathe. My meditation helped me gain perspective in an otherwise difficult work situation. Through it, I discovered gratitude for the co-workers I got to know better and for the income I received to support my daughters and myself during that period. Meditation helped me survive … and, eventually, thrive.

Problem-Solving Insights

Meditation brings a clear mental state for problem solving. When our problems seem insurmountable, a meditation practice helps filter out some of the junk. The "junk" may be our fears of what might happen, storylines from past experiences, and imagined conversations that have not taken place. A spiritual meditative space lets us see the actual facts more clearly and recognize our part in a situation. Meditation provides a deeper knowledge of potential solutions.

Patience

As you meditate, you learn to focus on your breath and the present moment. Because you're not projecting into the future, you'll find yourself becoming more patient and tolerant with others. If you continually get tangled up in drama and negativity, you hurt yourself both mentally and physically. When my day involves a "crisis" with my children, former spouse, telephone carrier, financial institutions, or other common stressors, meditation keeps me sane. By recognizing when your hand is caught in the jar, you learn to take a deep breath and let go sooner.

Learning to Release What You Can't Control

One of the trickiest challenges we face is to release our expectations of how other people should behave or how our lives should turn out. I like this quote, which I heard once: **"The only person I have to answer for on my deathbed is me."** For instance, you may feel aggrieved that a prior romantic partner cheated. You may feel hurt that your children lied to you about their activities. You may feel angry that your parents never understood you. You may dislike a boss who berates employees. While there may be healthy actions for you to take, you can't control other people. In such situations, you can set boundaries in your relationships and implement consequences for your children. You can try to communicate with your parents, and you can seek alternative employment. But ultimately, how these individuals live out their time on earth is not within your control. You can't control everything that happens at work, in your neighborhood, or across the globe. **Just do your part.** Focus on your breath, your heart, and your spirit. Whatever comes your way, remain loving and true to your path. **Surrender to a higher power all that you can't change in this lifetime.**

Try Optimism

It's said that you get what you look for. My mom's best friend, whom I considered an aunt, always saw the best in people. One time she placed an ad in the newspaper seeking her lost dog. A young man came to her door and said he'd seen the dog. My aunt offered to drive him to where he said he sighted the dog. She drove her car, as he directed, to a poor section of the city. Throughout the entire car ride, she told him what a wonderful person he was, how caring and thoughtful, and how incredibly grateful she was to him for his help. Eventually, the young man asked her to pull the car over; he got out and never came back. She waited—with no idea where she was or how to get back home. When a police officer came to assist her, he told her that she was lucky to be alive. She was in an extremely rough section of the city. I believe her seeing only the good in that young man may have saved her life.

Your attitude affects the quality of your life. When I maintain enthusiasm, I feel more joyful. Optimism doesn't always come easily for me when I get into worry mode. But I try to remind myself that sometimes all that is required is that I show up. We don't have to be perfect. And it's OK to make mistakes and start over. Optimism keeps us going during trying times. Consider how you feel—and the typical outcomes in your life—when you habitually feed your mind negative thoughts. Negative thoughts, despair, and hopelessness lead us down a destructive path. Negativity lowers your mood and your energy levels, along with making you less effective in achieving your life goals.

With children, optimism is especially valuable. Young minds carry the seeds planted by teachers, parents, caregivers, and relatives. Those seeds can take root and grow over the years. If you believe all children have gifts to offer, and if you communicate to children that they're special, they believe you. All children *are* gifted, talented, and blessed. People are like flowers, each contributing color and beauty to the planet and each blooming in their own unique ways.

Choosing optimism doesn't mean denying hardships. Contrary to popular belief, a spiritual life doesn't mean the absence of such challenges. You still mourn losses and acknowledge suffering. Optimism simply helps you continue on despite those trials. It keeps you focused on what you can accomplish—and not on what you can't change or control. I read somewhere that optimism is going to a disaster area and helping rebuild it, because **you believe in your power to make a difference in the world.**

Optimism recognizes that each day is a new beginning. There are so many unknown outcomes and unforeseen circumstances. Usually, there are options we never even considered. You might shift your mood or change your mind. You might realize your thoughts were mistaken. The entire culture or world may experience a positive shift. Tomorrow has not yet happened. Optimism asks, "What can I do today to make a difference in my life or in the life of someone I love?" When you reach out to help others, optimism puts your problems in proper perspective.

Whatever your life purpose, optimism helps align your thoughts with your highest aspirations. Spirit does not give up on us. We can seek out solutions. We can work on change. We can keep our thoughts on strength through Spirit or love's healing power. One quote I use from the Tao Ching is, "Do the work, set no store by it." While you can't control or predict outcomes, you remain responsible for your thoughts and deeds. Set your intentions. All flows from there.

We remain optimistic because we care about the future of our planet and the generations that come after us. We understand that our thoughts and actions influence more than our individual selves. **As Gandhi said, "You must not lose faith in humanity."**

Optimism Pointers:
- **Find one thing you are grateful for.**
- **List your positive intentions for a project, relationship, or your life.**
- **Remember: today is a brand new day.**

Affirmations, Slogans, and Quotes

It's easy to recognize how optimism might improve our lives. It's an entirely different matter to make optimism your daily practice. That's no simple task! Businesses spend billions of dollars on advertisements, often for products that convey a message that you're not OK as you are. Product advertisements promote the idea that you're not good enough, attractive enough, powerful enough, or smart enough ... unless you buy their car, cosmetics, clothing, deodorant, toothpaste, soft drink, etc. It takes tremendous awareness to counter these pervasive negative messages. Imagine if all those resources, talent, time, and energy went into creating a positive world image: A world where people of all shapes, colors, and sizes are considered beautiful.

When your mind starts down the slippery slope of despair, using positive affirmations, slogans, and quotes can pull your thoughts back from the brink. Such tools give you a way to reboot your thinking and put your mind on a more constructive path.

Affirmations are positive seeds that you plant in your mental garden. Even if you didn't receive encouraging seeds as a child, you can plant them now. They're declarations that something is so, even though you may not yet believe it. For instance, my affirmation is, "I am a gifted writer." I keep that affirmation in my journal for those days of self-doubt about my chosen work and my true calling.

When I returned to work after eight years of raising my children, my daily affirmation was "I refuse to let my job interfere with my joy." Affirmations are reminders of what's important to you. They gently hold your dreams and tell you to stay strong. Affirmations also set intentions. They are a way to say, "This is why I am here, even if other people do not yet support me in this effort." Affirmations push through doubts and fears. They remind you, "I am worthy. I am loved. I deserve joy and happiness. I am one with Spirit." They are the positive qualities your brain repeats so many times, until you understand that you are the affirmations. **You are what you believe yourself to be.**

Slogans are another way to move our lives in a more positive direction. Many sayings I use are from recovery programs. Alcoholics Anonymous, Al-Anon, and Alateen books provide daily readings with helpful slogans. Many of these sayings are found in other traditions and cultures as well. "First things first" and "Just for today" bring your thoughts to the present moment. "Live and let live," reminds us not to judge other people. "One day at a time" prevents us from spinning our mental chaos into a full-blown tornado. Some well-known proverbs have Native American origins: "Treat the earth well," "Don't judge your neighbor until you have walked two moons in his moccasins," "Walk in balance and beauty." Such sayings remind us of our higher intentions. They replace destructive thinking with life-affirming thoughts.

Quotes assist in a similar way by providing small doses of daily guidance. Consider these: "By their fruits ye shall know them," the Bible; "Imagination is more important than knowledge," Einstein; "The world is as you dream it," Shamanism. Quotes can serve as guideposts to direct your life. Useful quotes can be found in songs, poems, books, and movies. We adopted my daughter's favorite saying as a guiding quote: "In this family, we support each other's dreams." Even fortune cookies and tea bag quotes may prove helpful. One quote I like from a tea bag reads, **"Let your heart speak to others hearts."**

Find the affirmations, slogans, and quotes that bring strength for your journey and joy to your life. Place them somewhere visible or carry them with you. Write them in a journal each morning. Write them 15 or 20 times a day if necessary. Retraining your thinking takes time. It likely took many years to build your current thoughts, so be patient with the time it takes to adopt a set of positive beliefs.

Optimism Questions to Explore:
- **What affirmations, slogans, or quotes nourish my spirit?**
- **Which affirming thoughts do I want in my life?**

Prayers, Mantras, Inspirational Readings
Prayers, mantras, and inspirational readings help us with mental and spiritual attunement. Almost all faiths teach prayers of thanks. Mantras, in Hinduism, are sacred hymns or chants repeated in meditation. Phrases such as, "Om Mani Padme Hum," "Blessed are the Peacemakers," and "May all beings be filled with happiness" can

calm the mind. Repetitive prayers and mantras, like those repeated over a rosary (Roman Catholic beads) or mala (Hindu and Buddhist bead bracelets), put our minds in a receptive, meditative track. You don't have to be in a religious building to use prayers and mantras. Try repeating a mantra or prayer when walking, meditating, experiencing a rough patch in your day, or when beginning and ending your day. At night, I use prayers or mantras to move me into a more restful sleep mode. They give my brain permission to slow down, relax, and release the day's burdens.

Inspirational or devotional readings are another way to keep the mind on a spiritual track. These powerful sources of wisdom can be found in religious and spiritual texts, spiritual magazines, and online inspirational sites. **It's said that your mind can't hold two thoughts at the same time.** When you focus your attention on a reading that fills your mind with positive thoughts of love, kindness, and forgiveness, it becomes easier to expand those ideas into other areas of your life.

Prayers, mantras, and inspirational readings shift the internal stream of chatter into something that works better for your life. Making such mental choices doesn't mean you deny sad, angry, or frustrated feelings. These resources help you acknowledge those feelings and work through them. Some well-known prayers of strength and courage include: "Lord, make me a channel of your peace" (Saint Francis of Assisi), "When you are in doubt, be still and wait" (Ponca Chief White Eagle), "God, grant me the serenity to accept the things I cannot change" (Reinhold Niebuhr/Serenity Prayer), "Hold on to what you must do, even if it's a long way from here" (Pueblo Indian prayer). Such prayers acknowledge that you are feeling hurt and confused but are seeking guidance.

Try to keep an open mind and open heart toward prayers. Many years ago, a friend handed me a piece of paper right before I was about to give a public talk. The note read, "I can do all things through Jesus Christ who strengthens me." I read the prayer and thanked her but didn't believe that particular quote would help me. Years later, when I was in a situation where I thought I was dying, that phrase came back to me, along with a Native American song I had heard only once and visual images of strong women who had supported me in Goddess rituals years prior. (I discuss that event in more detail in Chapter 4). I don't know why these three particular sources came to me, but they provided comfort in a time of need, and I am extremely grateful that I didn't reject prayers that were offered with love. When I most needed strength, all those teachings resurfaced.

Remember, a prayer, mantra, or inspirational reading that worked for you may not be appropriate for someone else. I can't assume that I know what will best help another human, especially someone of a different culture, race, religion, or heritage. We all carry sources of wisdom. We can respect and honor other beliefs, even if we do not follow those teachings in our life.

As they say in indigenous societies and recovery programs, "Take only what you need and leave the rest." Teachings, doctrines, and religions point us in a certain direction. They are merely helpful paths—not the Source. In Buddhism it is said, "The finger pointing at the moon is not the moon." Meaning that religions and spiritual practices (like the pointing finger) are there to guide you. But your ultimate destination is Spirit, God, Universal Source, Goddess, Enlightenment, or whatever you seek (the moon).

Find the affirmations, slogans, quotes, mantras, prayers, and inspirational readings that assist you on your path. Put them where you can see them. We need daily reminders of our spiritual goals.

Each day brings new and unexpected situations. Our lives are interwoven with the many complexities that go with being alive and sharing space with other humans. Things don't always go as planned. People die, leave, and become ill. **The only constant, it is said, is change.**

Shifting into optimism takes mental dexterity and determination. Such work is not for the fainthearted. In the midst of human suffering, an affirmation, slogan, mantra, or prayer can offer spiritual sustenance to get you through another day.

Optimism Tips:
- **Write your affirmations/slogans/prayers/mantras in a daily journal.**
- **Post these sayings on the refrigerator.**
- **Write them on a chalkboard so you can change them as needed.**
- **Write them on tiny pieces of paper and carry them in your pocket.**
- **Write them with soap on your bathroom mirror.**
- **Give thanks for the blessings you receive.**

Healing Self-Talk
Healing self-talk directs your mind and heart toward a good path. Sometimes wounds we received early in life hang around into adulthood, interfering with our ability to have healthy relationships and to enjoy life. Unfortunately, we may still believe the negative messages we received from our teachers, parents, or peers.

When I was young, all the children in my grade school decided one morning that they should no longer talk to me because they thought I was ugly and not popular. Apparently, this type of shunning, particularly among groups of school age girls, was not uncommon at that time. I felt so incredibly sad by this "outcast" role that I left school for the rest of the day, saying I was sick. The next day, a couple of my best friends from the group said they didn't really mean it; they would still talk to me. Later, when this same sort of "group hate" happened to other girls, I was able to talk to the girls and let them know it would pass. But those hurt feelings go deep, even more so when other things in your family life are not going well. Out of the event, though, I developed enormous empathy for individuals who are treated unkindly by others.

Healing self-talk may entail revisiting yourself as a child and saying, "I am loved." So many of the wounds and suffering we carry as adults are a direct result of childhood traumas. A therapist once told me that if you have an extreme emotional reaction to a situation that ordinarily wouldn't warrant such a high level of heightened emotion, then it is likely related to something that occurred in childhood. **Healing those wounds becomes urgent on a spiritual journey to wholeness.**

I did an extremely helpful exercise in a meditation once for another childhood trauma. That childhood event involved finding my mother sprawled on the kitchen floor after she had taken an overdose of sleeping pills. I was very young at the time. Full of panic and anger, my stepfather screamed at me to "get out of the kitchen!" In my child's mind, I thought he was yelling at me for what had happened. Years later as an adult, a counselor suggested I revisit the attempted suicide scene again, during my meditation. This time, I placed white light around the event as I watched my parents and watched myself as a child. I saw my parents, as an outside observer, with sympathy. They seemed in so such turmoil. When I witnessed myself in the scene running up the hallway stairs and sitting down on a step to cry, I surrounded myself in compassion. In meditation, I could speak to the child and say, "Everything is going to be all right. You will get through this, and you're going to be OK." Ultimately, this meditative practice helped heal those wounds.

So much in life is a mystery. We don't know why certain things happened or did not happen. When we use healing self-talk, we take time to ask what we need to be whole, healthy, happy, and of service. Practice healing self-talk such as: "I am love. I release fear. I am healthy and whole." Then give thanks. "Thank you for love." Do not give up on life. Try reaching out to others who are suffering. Small acts lead to mighty results. A smile and 10-minute commitment to your happiness can redirect your life and your passion. Let down your walls, let in love, give love, let go of expectations, let go of outcomes, and embrace joy.

I've heard it said, **"God may have bigger plans for you than you have for yourself."** Another friend says, "God is protecting me from that person or situation," when things go in a direction she didn't anticipate. Nothing in this book is meant to deny suffering. Sometimes pain and suffering bring our greatest lessons. Developing compassion for other people's suffering, and the planet's suffering, leads to our individual and collective growth.

I once read that if you're experiencing suffering, put it to use. When my father died, an artist friend asked me, "Are you keeping a journal? Are you writing?" She understands that channeling our painful emotions into poems, songs, paintings, journal entries, music, scripts, acting, or storytelling is healing. Healing self-talk is essentially a focus on love and joy. Love and joy are powerful. When you learn to make these large and small shifts in your thinking, you begin to live more fully. Collectively, our decision-making skills also improve. When we align with love and positive alternatives, we expand our thinking and improve our lives.

Healing self-talk means aligning with Spirit in all aspects of your life. Even if professional therapy and prescribed medication are necessary for your mental, emotional, or physical well-being, healing self-talk adds to the effectiveness of medical approaches. If you aren't receiving positive and healthy talk from people in your workplace or in your home, practice your own healing self-talk. "Good job. I love you. I'm proud of you."

Negative talk is toxic. In unhealthy work environments, valuable employees quit or become physically ill. Abusive management styles may produce short-term results based on fear, but monetary gain is only one measure of "success." Long-term, the company as a whole will suffer. What is the measure of success when an employee commits suicide, suffers a heart attack, or goes through a divorce because he or she can't cope with unreasonable job demands? What's the measure of the company's success if you ask how many lives have suffered versus how many lives have benefited? This question doesn't apply only to human lives; it applies to all living organisms—animals, trees, plants, water, and Earth. If those organisms and elements suffer, we all suffer.

Workplaces can model healthy behavior for the individuals involved in the organization. The same is true in the family, committed relationships, community groups, faith-based organizations, and neighborhoods. Everyone can practice positive healing words. Abusive and hateful words are like poison. Healing communication is uplifting. "We can do it. You are so awesome. You are incredible." In your workplace, in your home, and in your mind, repeat phrases that affirm that you are worthy and loved. Remind yourself that your spirit and soul are special. **"God doesn't make junk" is a good motto to hold close to your heart.**

Changing Our Stories

The stories we tell ourselves influence our well-being. If your life story puts you in a victim role, then you may not feel empowered to make significant changes. Similarly, if your life story is that you have been fortunate or blessed, you may more readily recall the good things that have crossed your path. What is the theme of your life story? What common stories do you tell about your life? Here's what you need to know: **You are the author of your life story.** You can change your story and write one that will match your current desires and goals.

My story while growing up, for instance, was that my father left for Vietnam when I was 4 years old. He served a tour of duty in Vietnam, divorced my mother, and then returned to live in Vietnam as a civilian. My mother's story is that my father kidnapped me during child visitation and tried to take me with him on his return trip to live in Vietnam; my grandmother talked him into leaving me in the United States with my mother. As a teenager, my version of that story included images from movies such as "Apocalypse Now" and "The Deer Hunter." I felt intensely afraid of a man I assumed was mentally unstable. My storyline also included the core belief that my father didn't love me. By the time he returned to the United States and attempted to contact me, I was 16 years old and had built up so much fear that I refused to see him. Two decades later, when he died in a drunk driving accident, I revisited these family stories.

While attending my father's funeral as an adult, I received stories I never heard growing up. I found out that he had experienced childhood sorrows related to his father's death. I realized how young he and my mother had been when they married and I was born. More importantly, I discovered that he had loved me very much. I learned that sometimes people love us enough to want what is best for us, even if it means letting us go. I changed my story to one of forgiveness. My refusal to see him in my teens had hurt him, just as his absence from my life had hurt me. At his funeral service, I went outside for a while and stood in the sunlight. **Looking up at the sky, I made a bargain with the dead: "I'll forgive you, if you forgive me."**

It wasn't until his death that I finally felt his presence in my life. I wrote in my journal, I cried, and I communicated with him in prayer. I met the wife and family he brought back with him from Vietnam. He and that wife had also divorced, but I will never forget her kindness to me at the funeral. She told his now-adult children that I was his daughter, and she wrapped me under her arm like a lost lamb needing her protection. I will forever appreciate that kindness. In the process of learning more about my father's life, I was able to rewrite the stories in my head and release those long-held burdens.

Changing your life story may require gathering more information, gaining a different perspective, and forgiving human shortcomings. Your story should include your worthiness of love, regardless of how anyone else has behaved toward you. That may require developing compassion for those people who were not capable of showing love. Such people miss out on so much of life. You can change your stories to include a determination not to repeat past negative patterns. My personal story means I understand the value of telling young children how much they are loved. I recognize how important it is that my children spend time with their father, even after a divorce. I remember to love myself as best as I am able, despite outside circumstances.

These are not easy lessons. But harmful personal stories are worth exploring and rewriting. The facts may be harsh. The story may bring emotional suffering to the surface. But the deeper story, the heart story, is always about going forward in a way that brings you wholeness. As we share our stories, healing arrives. The mind and heart grow stronger. We can also explore our collective local and global stories. **We can always learn to heal and love, again.**

Laughter is the Best Medicine

Laughter is a tremendous healing tool. In times of stress, laughter relieves tension. A deep belly laugh can change your entire mood. It can also give you space to cope before you blow up or melt down. Comedy in the form of movies, jokes, and lighthearted attitudes helps lift your burdens. A funny joke may not solve all your problems, but it shows you another window to look out, at least momentarily.

Although tragedies of intense emotional suffering may block any ray of humor, sometimes these circumstances bring forth humor as an outlet to avoid a total breakdown. Have you ever laughed hysterically at a funeral when telling or listening to funny stories about the deceased? Uncontrollable laughter at funerals is not uncommon. There's a classic Mary Tyler Moore TV show about laughing at the funeral of Chuckles the clown. This behavior doesn't signify an absence of intense suffering. It simply means all barriers are down. What comes out in those situations is beyond rational control. Humor may be the release valve that bypasses some other intense emotional reaction, such as rage. Funerals often produce a range of emotional reactions, from laughing uncontrollably to lashing out angrily at someone or intensely sobbing.

With "minor" life events, humor puts things in perspective. You don't have to go to battle every time your spouse, co-worker, or neighbor acts in the way they typically act. A person who upsets you because he or she always behaves in a familiar way would not be the individual you know so well if he or she suddenly acted out of character. Gaining perspective allows you to see the humor in these situations. A child who is overly tired, for instance, is not intentionally making you crabby or annoyed. Humor in these circumstances may keep you sane for when the more serious events enter your life—and may help keep you sane in those times as well.

A lighthearted joke may soften bad news or acknowledge an outrageously crazy life event. Humor can say, in essence, **"We're all in this together."** When I returned to full-time work after my divorce, a co-worker often stopped by my office to offer a daily tidbit of wisdom. It was always something funny. At a time when I felt like my world was crashing, his two-minute "wisdom of the day" advice kept my spirit from sinking. You can't be overly absorbed in self-pity when you're laughing. As we all know, in many cases, things could be worse.

During holiday gatherings when I was young, my grandmother, aunts, and uncles used to gather around the dinner table and retell family stories until everyone was laughing so hard they cried or peed their pants. With my grandmother, the stories always told of tragedies. But with the 40-year gap in the telling, they sounded hilarious.

She would tell of the time my uncle accidentally set the house on fire and then, after they put the fire out, they lit it again because they were afraid the firefighters would show up and be angry if there wasn't a fire to put out. Or there was the time that the government gave my grandmother one school outfit per child. With no money, no husband, and five children, she lied and said someone stole all the clothes out of her car so she could get a second set of outfits for each child. Or the time they left their apartment in the middle of the night and moved into a vacant place across the street because they were behind on rent. The landlord moved new people into their old place and then, a few days later, the police came and evicted the new people. Or the time she sold a fur coat that she had gotten from the apartment of an evicted neighbor. She sold it for $25 to a woman who lived nearby. The woman came back demanding a refund when she realized that the entire back was filled with moth holes. My grandmother kept the money. She had five children to feed. They were living on cans of powdered milk and deliveries of chunks of cheese. All the kids developed rickets from malnourishment. To hear my grandmother tell these stories, you would think this family had the funniest and most enjoyable life on the planet. As my mother explains, "We didn't know we were poor. Everyone around us lived the same way."

My grandmother always maintained an upbeat attitude. Later, when she remarried and had extra money, she treated cash like candy freely handed out at Halloween. She made no distinction between 50 dollars and 5 dollars. If she had extra, she gave it away. Throughout her life, the theme of her stories remained: "Remember how crazy we were. We sure survived!" Even through extreme hardships, which included the death of her youngest son and the deaths of four grandchildren, my grandmother mastered this tool. She felt terrible grief over those losses, but she never complained. She told stories. She remembered those who died and all the funny and crazy things they did while alive. She loved fully and kept people alive in her stories. She never closed off her heart. **My grandmother laughed until she cried. Then she laughed some more because life is, after all, crazy.**

A friend of mine, Gayle Thundar, of the Miami Nation of Indians, told me the story of how her mother healed herself of cancer through laughter. The doctors told her mother that she had cancer and would need surgery within six months. Her mother went home and proceeded to watch funny movies. She never told anyone what she was doing. Other people's doubts and fears are not helpful when working on healing. When she went back to the doctors for her scheduled surgery, the cancer was gone. No one can explain it.

The next time your mood is low, rent a funny movie, enjoy a humorous book, or read the comics. Children's books and children's movies cheer me up when I'm feeling down. My daughters and I used to love reading Shel Silverstein's *Where the Sidewalk Ends*, and Dr. Seuss' *The Cat in the Hat*. Funny books and movies can help us see the absurdity of the human condition. Use your mind to laugh at yourself and others, with love and tenderness. Remember funny stories and share them with others. Those people who bring levity and humor into our homes, workplaces, and communities should be thanked profusely for sharing that magnificent gift.

CHAPTER 3

BODY: Exploring Your Life's Dance

"I finally discovered the source of all movement,
the unity from which all diversities of movement are born."
—Isadora Duncan, dancer

Your body holds amazing abilities. It can be used to develop greater mental, physical, and spiritual balance. At times, your body is more revealing than your thoughts about how you feel or what you're experiencing. For instance, your mind may rationalize why you shouldn't be angry, or it may deny that something is bothering you. But a stiff neck, headache, or upset stomach won't let you hide those feelings for long.

By listening to your body, you can explore helpful questions in your self-discovery. If you feel your chest getting tight or your heart rate speeding up, for example, you can ask: "Am I afraid? What is it I fear? What do I need to feel safe?" Similarly, when you feel loving or happy, pay attention to how your body feels. Observe the thoughts and internal shifts influencing your physical reactions. Take a physical inventory the next time you're feeling angry or stressed. What happens in your body? Write down where you physically feel the emotion. Do you feel it in your chest? In your heart? In your head? In your throat? With a physical inventory, you'll learn how your body behaves under certain emotional conditions. You can then address what needs to change in your thinking or in the situation before the stress or anger gets out of control.

If your body shows signs of being out of balance, it may be giving you clues to internal emotional issues or external circumstances needing your attention. On the other hand, when your mind is calm and centered, and your emotions are fluid, you may experience increased health, vitality, and energy. Many books and research studies have documented the connections between our mind, emotions, and physical health. A study at Duke University found that exercising three times a week assists with reducing the impact of major depression. Research has also demonstrated that meditation boosts immune functions. Other research studies have linked chronic stress to high blood pressure, heart disease, indigestion, and migraines. Studies of post-traumatic stress disorder further illustrate how extreme stress can harm emotional, physical, and mental health.

Working with the subtle energies of the body teaches you how to make physical, mental, and spiritual adjustments when necessary. Fortunately, there are tools to assist with this process.

Let Your Body Guide You

Body movement methods have been used for centuries as a form of energy awareness, improved health and vitality, and prayer. Yoga, T'ai Chi, and Qigong, plus Sufi and Native American dance rituals, integrate physical, mental, and spiritual wellness. Many hospitals, medical facilities retirement homes, indigenous communities, health practitioners in Eastern cultures, and alternative healing centers utilize body energy practices for people with various physical, mental, and emotional health ailments.

Yoga

Yoga is now widely recognized in the West. Originating in India, it was brought to the United States by Hindu teachers. Today, the yoga commonly practiced in the West is known as Hatha yoga. These physical postures restore balance and increase the energy flow through the body. Yoga works on many levels to connect mind, body, and spirit. Practicing yoga is a spiritual undertaking and not merely a physical workout.

I discovered yoga during my divorce. I had moved into a new neighborhood, and a friend mentioned that a neighbor offered yoga classes in her home—in a beautiful room that overlooked a river. For this teacher, Lee Edgren, yoga instructions are not an exercise routine. She teaches her classes with a spiritual focus, which includes gentle meditation time. Teaching and practicing yoga is her life purpose.

The yoga poses provided me a sense of both physical and emotional strength. I began to notice where in my body I carry tension. I realized that I experience pain in my neck and lower back when I feel stressed. At those times, it feels like I'm carrying the weight of the world. **Yoga kept my spirit from giving up.**

After moving out of my marital home, it took me nine months to find employment. I faced extreme financial pressures. I worried about the effect of the divorce on my children; I worried about my personal failings; and I worried about the loss of community and friendships as a result of my relocation. Yoga gave my mind and body a safe space while I worked through those emotional and financial hardships. My body needed a way to release internal mental and emotional constraints. Yoga served as a gateway to let those worries out! By releasing worries, stress, anxiety, depression, sadness, and grief related to the divorce, my body, mind, and spirit began to feel lighter.

A yoga practice shows you where you hold resistance and possibly what struggles or challenges you're facing in this life's journey. It is also a meditative practice. Focusing on an unfamiliar body position forces your mind to pay attention. When combining body, breath, and movement, you must concentrate fully on the moment at hand. If you're holding a physical pose and paying attention to your breathing, you don't have much extra space for mental chatter.

Yoga can be wonderfully self-empowering. Gaining flexibility in your body may help you bend more easily in other areas of your life, and strengthening your body may help you grow stronger in some aspects of your life. Yoga teaches the body how to stretch and then relax and how to stay strong yet supple. The poses demonstrate how to maintain balance and how to make minor or major adjustments to regain your balance when you falter. More importantly, you begin to slow down. Yoga gives the mind a resting place in the midst of a storm. Positive energetic movement occurs in the body, mind, and spirit. All are in harmony.

Yoga classes are available for both children and adults. When they were young, my daughters enjoyed a fun children's DVD: *YogaKids*.® The video uses animals and music to engage young children in the poses. Find a yoga class near you or rent a high-quality video—one that treats yoga as a spiritual activity. Once you learn a few basic yoga positions, you can practice at home or even at work on your break if you have appropriate space (and an understanding boss). Loose clothing, a mat, and a willing spirit are all that is required for most classes.

T'ai Chi

T'ai Chi is an ancient Asian meditative body practice that combines a focus on breath, movement, energy, and harmony of spiritual and physical health. T'ai Chi teaches how to sense chi (life force or universal energy) flowing through your body and all around you.

I met my T'ai Chi teacher, Jeff Tessler, at an annual gathering for local writers. I don't recall what his connection was to that event, but the instructor offered to take some of us outside and teach us a couple of movements. I was so inspired by that brief lesson that I signed up for an eight-week course, even though I had never before heard of T'ai Chi. I found out later that my instructor is a master level teacher. His teachings were passed down through a lineage of master teachers and he received permission from his teacher to pass on the T'ai Chi lessons. **As they say, when you're ready, the teacher arrives.** If a learning opportunity presents itself to you, stay open and receptive. It could prove worthwhile.

T'ai Chi classes consist of learning the physical movements and mindfully practicing them. T'ai Chi is another method for slowing down, becoming more aware of your body, and sensing the physical and energetic movements through space. T'ai Chi is a good metaphor for life: We are often in continual motion, but we need to be intentional in our actions and aware of how those actions may affect the world. As we breathe and move, we remain mindful of what we are doing in each moment.

Such awareness influences how you interact with others. Groups, places, and people all emit various energy vibrations. When you start to sense your energy or another person's energy, you learn not to let someone else's mood control your day. You recognize which situations help you feel vitalized and which cause you to feel drained.

Becoming aware of these positive and negative energy levels helps you make wise choices as you move forward on your life path.

Qigong

The practice of Qigong is an ancient Chinese healing art involving meditation, controlled breathing, and body movements. The first time I heard of Qigong was on a family vacation during a stressful stage in my first marriage. At that time, my husband and I had two young children, and we were frequently fighting or emotionally withdrawn from each other. A group of people from our religious organization had joined together for a weeklong vacation at a lakeside resort. Being on vacation in such a beautiful setting while we were estranged only enhanced my feelings of isolation and loneliness.

One afternoon while I was eating lunch in the cafeteria, my husband came in to announce that he and my friend were going to play tennis, and he needed me to watch our children. The friend and her family had joined us from the East Coast on this trip. I had not spent any time with my husband or my friend. I felt resentment, sadness, and burdened with childcare responsibilities during what was supposed to be our vacation. As I chewed my food, I silently churned through these emotions. Because my husband and I were not spending any enjoyable time together, the deepest feeling was intense loneliness. We had gotten to a point in our relationship where we simply took turns minding our young children, separately.

An older woman sitting across the lunch table from me intuitively picked up on my sadness. When my husband left the cafeteria, she asked if I would like to learn some Qigong movements. She explained that after she had lost her husband to brain cancer, she met with a master Qigong teacher to help her work through her grief. Despite having no idea what she was going to teach me, I agreed.

After lunch, she and I walked to the lake dock where she showed me three very simple Qigong movements. One involved gently rocking back and forth on the heels of my feet with my eyes closed. Another involved arm and hand motions that gently thump the heart. All the while, I looked out over a lake shimmering in the bright summer sun.

When our session ended, I walked over and sat down on a nearby bench. Nothing externally had changed, yet I felt calmer. Shortly thereafter, my husband came by. He said he had been thinking about the afternoon plans, and he could watch the children after his tennis match so that I could have some relaxation time. Our marriage didn't resolve its many problems. But for that moment, I felt happier. It was like a small window in my heart had opened enough to let in a soft breeze. Somehow, my heart opening—even slightly—had altered my perception of the afternoon. Instead of carrying anger and blame, I felt peaceful. Such small shifts can make a difference.

Even today, many years later, I still practice those Qigong movements. They remind me of the balance and harmony within myself and the energetic harmony that touches everything in an imperceptible yet positive way.

Dances of Universal Peace and Native American Dances

In many spiritual and religious traditions, dancing is a form of prayer. It is also an enjoyable method for raising energy awareness.

Sufi dance is based on Sufism, the mystical tradition of Islam. The thirteen-century Persian Sufi, Jalaluddin Rumi, inspired a ritual whirling dance. In the West, these dancers are often referred to as whirling dervishes.

Unlike the whirling dervishes, the Sufi dances I have attended are called Dances of Universal Peace. Samuel L. Lewis introduced the Dances of Universal Peace in the 1960s. Hazrat Inayat Khan, who brought Sufism to the West from India, and Ruth St. Denis, a modern dance pioneer in America and Europe, influenced Sam's teachings.

My experience with these dances took place with instructor Paula Sapphire, who teaches at Butler University and holds Dances of Universal Peace in her home. She also holds these dances at various religious organizations. For some of my friends, Sufi dancing is their sole spiritual practice. The dances are a way to pray and directly connect with Spirit. The Dances of Universal Peace are simple, repeated movements that are taught to the participants. The dances are intended to be inclusive and open to anyone. With Dances of Universal Peace, a deep connection and interaction with others is part of the group's spiritual experience. The Sufi dances are a way of bringing people together and having a method to worship that uses sacred phrases and melodies from different spiritual traditions.

American Indian dance ceremonies are another example where dancing is a form of prayer. These dances involve sacred teachings, prayer songs, drumming, and traditional ceremonial dress. Participants perform specific rituals in preparation for the dances. The dancers may have gone on Vision Quests, made tobacco prayer bundles, and participated in sweat lodge ceremonies. Community support is an integral part of the dance ceremonies. Everyone contributes in some way during ritual dancing. For these dances, honoring sacred traditions is central to the ceremony.

As such, the dances and other rituals are not open to outsiders. Historically, European settlers did not respect, understand, or honor these traditions. Even today, prayers and sacred traditions from American Indian tribes are not often revered. Perhaps visitors will be welcomed when these dances are given the same value as a prayer spoken in a house of worship.

I have attended Indian dance ceremonies in Colorado. I went at the invitation of a fire keeper. I stayed only after receiving approval from the person holding these sacred dances. A fire keeper is a person who literally keeps the fire burning during the dance. At these dances, I was exposed to meaningful ceremonies that contained so much more than simply a dance. The dances are intertwined with nature, prayers, sky, dancers, drummers, supporters, sun, birds, creatures, trees, Earth, ancestors, healing, gratitude, children, and Creator. **All one. All connected.**

Prior to my time in Colorado, I had never felt a desire to attend Native American dance ceremonies. I didn't know they existed. The invitation came to me; I did not seek it out. When the person I was dating urged me to attend, my motive was to be open to Spirit. It was never for self-gain or exploitation of a culture or a people. These dance ceremonies were some of the most profound experiences of my life. I am extremely grateful for my time there and for the generous, thoughtful, and kind-hearted people I met.

After a couple of years, it became clear that my physical presence at these ceremonies had come to an end. This knowing came about through guided dreams and changed circumstances. In my dream, the ceremony participants turned their backs to me. Additionally, I was no longer dating the person who had introduced me to the ceremonies. I wasn't pleased with that outcome, but when Spirit speaks there's likely a reason—even if the reason isn't immediately understood. Apparently, I had more learning waiting for me elsewhere. For the American Indian teachings, however, I remain forever indebted. My Spirit soars with thanks like a great bird that now has wings.

While most Native American ceremonies are private, Pow Wow gatherings are frequently open for respectful observation by the general public. If you have an interest in this area, ask for teachings from someone of American Indian ancestry, visit a Pow Wow, or seek on-line resources for tribal education centers.

Trust Your Senses

Your senses are useful guideposts on your journey to wholeness. When you pay attention to input from your sense of sight, sound, touch, smell, and taste, you receive insights. We all know that our senses can alert us to danger. We might observe movement in a nearby alley, hear unfamiliar clanging, feel a tingling on our skin, smell smoke, or taste the pungent sourness of spoiled food. If one or more of your senses is impaired, your other senses are likely stronger than average. These same senses that help us navigate our physical life can also point us toward greater spiritual awareness. We may just need a little practice picking up the signals.

Experiment to find the mix that works for you. For instance, taking a hot bath, smelling lavender soap, and then listening to Pachelbel's Canon while sipping chamomile tea might bring you an hour of serenity. Or perhaps smelling pine, hearing the snow crunch under your boots, feeling a cold breeze, and watching the early morning sunrise gets you in tune with Spirit. **Utilize your senses to bring about desired life changes.**

Sight

Artists are an excellent resource for the visual components in our lives. They typically study how colors, textures, shapes, and images evoke certain moods or elicit specific emotions. Advertisers spend billions using visual images to influence emotions, thoughts, and behavior. Learning what visuals assist you on your path is a positive use of this knowledge.

A fun, low-cost way to experiment with desired life changes is through colors. Discover which colors resonate with you and which you typically avoid. A hint of red or purple may bring confidence during a job interview, yellow flowers may cheer up a gloomy day, and a vast blue sky may bring calm. Green or blue may produce peaceful feelings; red may bring a sense of passion or romance; purple may empower your sense of royalty or wisdom; orange may inspire creative energy; and black may represent formality, authority, mystery, or grief.

Colors signify different things, depending on cultural and religious heritages. In some Native American tribes, white on the medicine wheel symbolizes North, purity, and wisdom. In Asian cultures, white may symbolize funerals and death. In Western cultures, it can symbolize a bride or peace. In Goddess traditions, white may symbolize pure spirit. Depending on your beliefs, red may represent Earth, East, fire, anger, power, passion, authority, compassion, death, or love. Native American tribes, Goddess traditions, Christian churches, Buddhist and Hindu sects and other religious organizations frequently associate symbolic meaning with the colors chosen for their robes, candles, religious paintings, prayer flags, prayer wheels, prayer beads, medicine wheels, artifacts, and mandalas.

Explore what meaning colors hold for you. Try bringing new colors into your life. Add to your life those colors that bring you peace and joy.

Sight Questions to Ask:

- **What do the colors of my religious, spiritual, or cultural heritage signify?**
- **What colors help me feel strong, brave, spiritually centered, or cheerful?**

Visual images likewise influence mood and emotions. If nature scenes prompt you to feel more relaxed, display a nature calendar in your office or hang some photos of flowers, trees, and sunsets. Maybe you draw inspiration from renowned spiritual leaders? If so, pictures of Dr. Martin Luther King Jr., Gandhi, Jesus, Buddha, or Mother Teresa may keep you motivated when the world feels overwhelming. Or perhaps a child's painting taped to your door will remind you to stay lighthearted as you begin your day. Animal pictures can also serve as inspiration. A kitten may convey gentleness, a black panther may encourage strength, and a hummingbird may be a reminder of joy.

Visuals are powerful. Chose those images that offer meaning to your life and put them where you can see them daily.

Feng Shui

Feng Shui is the Chinese art of harmonizing with our environment. Have you ever noticed how some buildings or homes feel incredibly hectic and other places feel more peaceful?

According to the principles of Feng Shui, as applied to your living environment, the physical arrangement and elements within your home or office influence the balance or imbalance of the energy in that space. With elements (wood/metal/water/earth/fire), you can create various effects. For example, you can discern if you prefer wood floors because they feel calming. Perhaps you like silver and chrome modern fixtures that produce high energy. Do you enjoy water fountains because they are soothing, or is digging in the garden your calming activity? Maybe your favorite pastime is sitting near a fireside hearth. These are examples of how those elements can affect mood.

Those who practice this art study the physical components, elements, and energetic aspects of a living or working space. Beyond the home, Feng Shui principles apply to garden and outdoor spaces, relationships, health, career, eating habits, and so on. In modern Western culture, we primarily apply this art to our homes and businesses. There are many factors that influence the flow of energy in these environments: lighting, objects, shapes, colors, directions, entryways, building materials, layout, and more.

A former minister at a Unitarian Universalist church I attended asked a friend to give a Feng Shui consultation for his office so that the space would feel comfortable when church members came to him for pastoral care. Having witnessed the space before and after, I can say that changes based on the Feng Shui evaluation made a significant difference. The room felt more open, inviting, and softer than it had before.

Feng Shui adjustments to your home don't demand great wealth and excessive material possessions. Improvements to make your space feel more serene might be as simple as lining your window ledge with stones or moving a chair closer to a window that faces south. The loving and mindful attention you give your physical environment is what makes it peaceful—not the money you spend. You can also open up space in your life by cleaning out junk that has accumulated in drawers, rooms, closets, sheds, and garages. Allow more room for what truly pleases your senses.

Even if you live in a small apartment or rent a single room, it is still your living space. Young people do much to claim their bedrooms or college dormitory rooms as their own. They intuitively find ways to add their own personal flair to these spaces—and most do so without spending a lot of money. While you may not want to adopt the stereotype of the messy teenager's bedroom, don't let the size of your space inhibit your Feng Shi efforts to harmonize your area.

Creating an Altar

To bring sacred space into your life, you can also set up an altar in your home. An altar serves as a visual reminder of your spiritual or religious path. If you plan to use your altar as a sanctuary for your spiritual practice, there are some household factors you may want to consider as you select the location.

Altar Location Considerations Include:
- **Quiet**
- **Privacy (is the area heavily traveled by other members of the household)**
- **Access to sunlight (if that is important to you)**
- **Comfort of space for sitting or kneeling (if that is part of your spiritual practice)**

Once you determine the location, choose an area for displaying your sacred objects. You can use a table, bookshelf, desktop, cloth spread out on the floor, fireplace mantel, spot at the base of a tree, or any other area that fits with your living arrangements. Select those objects that remind you of your path. They could be photographs of your ancestors, items that symbolize your highest aspirations, candles, pictures of loved ones, or religious artifacts. You could include a statute of the Buddha, a cross or rosary, the Serenity prayer, a Goddess figurine, a feather, or a picture of a saint, guru, or spiritual leader you admire.

Even if you have no particular religious affiliation, you can set up an altar that holds significance for you. I know someone who has a crayon on his altar to remind him of his desire for childlike playfulness. Objects from nature such as stones, leaves, or shells can be extremely spiritual. There is no right or wrong. Be creative. Simply think about what your altar represents for you.

Consider These Questions For Your Altar:

- **Do I want my altar to remind me of life's beauty and joy?**
- **What images remind me of the importance of my spiritual work?**
- **What represents ways in which my spiritual path has meaning for me?**

Visuals Outside the Home

Even in a workplace, hospital, or prison setting, you may be able to find a tiny corner for visually healing images. An inspirational quote taped to your wall, for example, may soothe your spirit. A calming image on your computer screen saver or a prayer tucked in your wallet can remind you that you are on a spiritual journey. Your inner soul work continues no matter where you physically find yourself. **Your real daily work is with your heart, mind, and spirit.**

Your workplace may provide challenges and opportunities for growth, or it may be a toxic environment that you need to vacate. In either case, you are learning what you need and what your spirit needs for wholeness. In whatever setting you find yourself, you have an opportunity to learn what gifts you bring to others and what gifts they bring to you. A friend of mine wrote about his mother's kindness toward each person who entered the hospital room during her treatments for leukemia. I've also met a man on Death Row who, despite his circumstances, was devoting his time to personal and spiritual growth.

If you're in a location without access to any visual images, then your visual imagery may have to come from your memory or be created in your imagination. You only need call up one small seed from your memory to remind you of beauty. The image may be something you recall from childhood, such as a peaceful location or helpful person. Visualize one moment in your life that gave you a sense of well-being. If no visual comes to mind, use your imagination to create one. In a calm meditation, place yourself in a beautiful, relaxing, and safe space. You can visualize mountains, waterfalls, meadows, or trees—whatever helps you feel peaceful. Visualize yourself surrounded by light and love. Visit this imagined place whenever needed. **No one is in charge of your thoughts**. Take them where they need to go to regain your sense of Spirit's loving embrace.

Symbols

Symbolic images are valuable visual tools for healing. A mandala, for instance, is a form of sacred art. It usually contains a square border, an inner circle with symmetrical shapes, and a central focus point. The Buddhist sand mandalas are famous for their intricacy, brilliant colors, and impermanence. They are used as a meditative and spiritual teaching tool. Within the mandala may be images of temples, animals, deities, nature, geometric shapes, and so on. The images may tell a story, show a path to enlightenment, provoke a contemplative state, or provide a means of healing. Paradoxically, a mandala focuses the mind outward on the images while simultaneously bringing your attention inward.

What you observe in symbols may not make sense in logic or words. With symbolic images, you access the subconscious. Tarot cards and religious symbols work in a somewhat similar way by communicating messages to your inner self from the meanings attached to the images. Depending on your religious background, trees may symbolize ancient wisdom. A dove may denote peace. A dragon may signify creativity. A coiled snake may symbolize healing in the medical profession, the kundalini (life force energy) in Hinduism, or fertility in the Goddess traditions. Shapes also hold meaning. A cross may represent sacrifice. Predating Christianity, an Egyptian cross with a loop may represent everlasting life or the Goddess Sekhmet. A spiral is meaningful for those who follow Goddess traditions. A circle (hoop) holds significant meaning for Native American tribes.

Symbols speak in powerful and lasting ways. You can use symbolic imagery to reinforce your deepest spiritual beliefs. And if you wish to reject certain symbols because they no longer fit your belief system, you can certainly do so. Many women are reclaiming ancient symbols that represent the Feminine Divine in their spirituality. As we increase our knowledge, we might adopt or create new symbols that more truly embody our path.

Creative Visual Expression

Art therapy can be extremely beneficial for emotional healing. It enables a free expression of fears, anger, and emotional pain as well as joys, miracles, and celebrations. Cancer patients, for instance, may draw or paint their healing images while also expressing their sorrows. With art, people can openly and honestly share their concerns, hopes, and desires. It's empowering to pick up a paintbrush, marker, or crayon and pour out emotions that are bottled up inside. It can also be surprising to discover what lies dormant in the hidden recesses of the wounded heart. A brush of vibrant yellow paint on a dark canvas or a splattering of red on a white canvas may speak volumes if you are working on grief and healing.

The next time you're processing difficult emotions, try using paint, crayons, markers, chalk, clay, or fabric to express what can't easily be put into words. Make a collage with magazine pictures, glitter glue, plastic stars, and construction paper. A collage can display your goals, dreams, and visions. It might contain images that illustrate a healthy, happy, and loving life. I've used collages to envision the type of home I wanted, to remind myself of the causes that are important to me, and to point me toward spiritual paths I wish to someday travel.

Creativity opens the gateway for understanding and release. Through art, you tap deeper levels of consciousness and enormous emotional reservoirs beyond the grasp of words. We learn what lies beneath our job titles, roles, and labels. Like young children, we begin to freely display what is in our hearts—with colorful scribbles that go outside the lines. **We discover that suffering, beauty, and joy exists within, only waiting to be expressed.**

Sound

Sound greatly influences our feelings of wellness. Whether through music, conversation, or quiet reflection, the sounds we hear and the sounds we convey influence the peacefulness of our inner and outer environments. Harsh sounds easily cause agitation and annoyance. Soft, quiet music often helps us relax.

Vibrational sound affects not only people but also plants and animals. An article in Integrative and Comparative Biology, a journal published by the Oxford University Press, describes how various species use vibrations for mating, to detect predators and locate prey, and to relay information. (See "Vibration and Animal Communication: A Review" by Peggy S.M Hill [2001]). In 1973, Dorothy Retallack published a seminal book, *The Sound of Music and Plants*, indicating how continuous tones harm plant growth. But more than likely, no one has to prove to you that after a full day of noisy children, incessant construction hammering, or a neighbor's loud music, you feel agitated and fatigued. We already know sounds affect our well-being. On a spiritual path, we can use that information to our benefit.

Music

Movies are one example where music is used to arouse strong emotions. A melancholy song during a love scene or death scene—when done well—can bring us to tears. Music at funerals is another situation where sounds cause an outpouring and release of intense emotions. We hear a song that the deceased person loved, and it immediately brings that person to mind, along with all the memories associated with the person.

Once when I was a teenager, I was driving along in my Impala, listening to an oldies station on the radio, and I heard a Simon and Garfunkel song, Cecilia. I was sitting at a red light near my house, singing along with the song, and I suddenly remembered the scene where my mother had attempted suicide (discussed earlier in the section on Healing Self-Talk). What is significant here is that I had blocked that memory for over a decade. My mom loved listening to Simon and Garfunkel, and I must have associated that song with her. Music retrieved a memory that I had unknowingly blocked. I drove home and confirmed with her that yes, when I was extremely young, she had taken an overdose of sleeping pills. Even though painful, remembering helped me eventually work on healing that deep wound.

Those working in the field of music and sound therapy recognize that music promotes healing. Research indicates it can ease stress, anxiety, depression, and anger. Music and sound vibrations are used in various medical fields, such as working with autistic individuals. It is also effectively used in religious and spiritual healing rituals.

During my lunch break at work one day, I visited a nearby church for some quiet reflection time. The organist was rehearsing on the second level, and cavernous, melodic sounds filled the sanctuary. As I sat listening, I suddenly found myself weeping. I had not fully realized how my workday stress and emotional exhaustion were affecting me. I let the tears flow down my face. I could not pinpoint the exact source of my sadness at the time. Some days, just observing the world around us can be a challenge: The indifference, the waste, the lack of simple kindness, and the excess of ego can wear us down. We need ways to release all the unhealthy toxins we take in each day. Sound helps with that process.

There are positive stories of musicians invoking the universal language of music during wars and catastrophes. It is a tool capable of crossing ethnic, religious, cultural, and language barriers. Once, while visiting Prague in the Czech Republic, I was strolling along a bridge where artists were displaying their paintings and sketches. Suddenly, a loudspeaker announced a bomb threat on the bridge. Everyone had to immediately clear the bridge. A woman in a nearby grassy area, in a language I didn't recognize, sat singing and playing a guitar. Even though I couldn't understand the words of the song, I felt calmer. Later that evening, I listened as a man stood under a lamppost and played the violin—his music floating beautifully through the night sky. **It was a glorious gift he offered freely to all within hearing.**

Sometimes we're not aware of all the sorrows, stress, and joy within us. Music taps into these hidden reservoirs. You can play soothing music to quell an anxious mind, upbeat music to lift your spirits, and melancholy music to release pent-up sadness. If you feel fearful, or if you received a lot of negativity from someone, music can shift your thoughts and emotions to a calmer state. Chants and repetitive melodic notes can put you in an altered state and help you become more receptive to spiritual guidance. Singing bowls, chimes, and bells are universal sound vibrations that communicate the need for a pause, a breath, or a prayer. Melodic sounds in nature—crickets chirping, rippling streams, birds twittering, and the wind rustling the leaves—can also soothe our spirits. The sound of hummingbird wings, the rhythmic thrum of cicadas, or the drum of a woodpecker can show us more life and activity in the world than our own direct situation.

Your body takes in a tremendous amount of information from your sensory environment. Be sure you are intentional about what your body and spirit absorb. Also, notice what vibrations you put out into the world. Your words, your thoughts, and your actions all carry their own vibrations. When you vibrate inner peace, the life that extends outward from there is more peaceful. In addition, some belief systems say that the vibrations we send out attract those same vibrations back to us. Said another way, what you give comes back to you tenfold. But even if you don't believe that maxim to be true, it is true that **you are responsible for what you put into the world, regardless of anyone else.**

Listening

Paying attention to what we hear through language is one way we learn. Whether it's a conversation with your child or a dialogue with a partner, co-worker, or neighbor, listening is a critical life skill. When we remain receptive, we often hear exactly what we need to hear—that bit of wisdom that moves us along our path. But you can't listen carefully or learn what's needed if you're talking, interrupting, judging, planning your rebuttal, or mentally wandering away from what the person is saying. When you listen from the heart, you are better able to speak from your heart. The exchange is then healthier, less antagonistic, and less focused on accusations, putdowns, sarcasm, and blaming.

Truly listening requires practice. One way to get the practice is to have a method in place that reinforces listening over talking. In meditation groups, there is often what is called a dharma topic for discussion—usually these topics are related to Buddhist principles and practices. Before speaking, a person bows. All other participants bow to acknowledge the person who will speak. While someone is speaking, no one else talks. They simply listen. When the person is done speaking, he or she bows to show that they are finished. Recovery groups also have guidelines against "crosstalk"—meaning you do not interrupt, give advice, or speak to someone else's issues. When it's your turn to speak, you only speak from your personal experience and for what is true in your heart. In a Wisdom Circle, you pick up a stone, feather, or other object from the center when you wish to speak and then replace it when you're finished. Only the person holding the object speaks; everyone else listens. These are good practices for creating a safe, listening environment.

Nonviolent communication workshops are another avenue for gaining tools that build healthier communication skills. These workshops emphasize speaking only to your own feelings and needs. The idea is to recognize that we share common needs. When we understand these core needs (such as a need for safety, trust, and love), we can listen more carefully and speak more authentically to the issues at hand.

Create your own listening methods with loved ones and friends. For instance, you might light a candle and say a prayer before having a difficult dialogue with someone. You can set aside a day and time for allowing the other person to talk, while you listen without interruptions or judgments. But be warned: This process requires work. That's why it's so important to practice. Through practice, we learn to understand where the other person is coming from and where our views are mistaken. We learn to develop compassion for the other person's struggles. And we begin to notice our storylines—those themes and stories in our lives that we keep repeating. Stories such as, "No one understands me," or "No one cares about my feelings," or "I have to do everything." These stories may not have anything to do with the facts at hand. They're just stories. For example, someone may not keep plans for getting together with you. The fact that this person didn't keep his or her plans does not mean, "Nobody cares about my feelings." As another example, if my husband reads the newspaper after we have a disagreement, it does not necessarily signify, "He doesn't love me." That type of "time-out" may be his coping mechanism and have nothing to do with his love for me.

With increased listening skills, you'll discover wisdom from family members, strangers you meet in your daily interactions, and even young children. I was at a restaurant with my daughter one afternoon casually telling her about a massage appointment I'd scheduled for myself later that day. I started to order coffee from the waitress, and my daughter said, "If you're going for a massage, you shouldn't drink coffee. That's artificial energy." She was young, but she was correct. You can't always anticipate who has information that will be useful to your learning or helpful to your life circumstances. **Sometimes knowledge comes from the least likely sources.** My hairdresser, children, co-workers, and new acquaintances have often surprised me with helpful tidbits of wisdom.

If your mind and ears are closed, you'll miss what someone has to teach. When you listen to others, you're taking in their sacred stories, their pain, and their suffering. Hold that knowledge close to your heart, not carelessly passing judgment or interrupting. Listen for the wisdom. You can learn through silent receptivity. If you're sincere in your seeking and using your heart as your guide, what you need will come. You don't have to force it. When you give someone your presence and your attention, you convey to them that they matter. You don't have to change someone else. Listening without judgment also alleviates much stress. You can let go of the need to do anything more.

Listening Tips:

- **Repeat back what you think you heard someone say.**
- **Don't make assumptions.**
- **Ask questions to clarify.**
- **Try not to judge, blame, or criticize what someone has said.**

Touch

Many years ago, I watched a disturbing movie entitled *Crash* where people's lives collided in unexpected and often negative ways. After the movie, I remember thinking that we needed to have more healthy touch in our culture. Despite all the sensationalized emphasis on sex, our culture is touch deprived. Where do we go for physical comfort after the death of a spouse, a divorce, or loss of a child? Where do we find caring, nonsexual physical contact? Some school systems actually forbid teachers from touching their students, even though a warm hug may be exactly what their students need.

We all desire loving human connection. Fortunately, even when living alone, there are methods for adding healing touch to your life.

Massage

Massage is an excellent way to give or receive physical touch without sexual content. A massage relaxes the body, releases toxins, and reduces stress. Along with personal massages, a massage can also serve people in need of healing touch in nursing homes and hospitals.

When the body fully relaxes, the mind soon follows. You are less likely to mull over worries and feel stressed when your entire body is calm. Relaxation can also shift consciousness. We feel better. Life seems less problematic, less complicated. We are then better able to offer that calm peace to others.

There are various types of massages, including deep muscle, reflexology, and Swedish—to name only a few! Workout facilities and gyms frequently offer appointments with massage therapists. Some massage therapists even have offices in busy downtown buildings where overworked and overstressed individuals can relax for a 20-minute or hour-long massage. You can also give a back massage, hand massage, or foot rub to your family members. Soft music, incense, hot towels, and oils can help relax the body during a massage. Physically relaxing reminds you to breathe slower and appreciate the moment. Healing of body, mind, and spirit work together. **When you heal on one level, you benefit the interrelated parts of your whole being.**

Reiki

Reiki is a healing touch method attributed to the teachings of Mikao Usui, a Japanese Buddhist. Reiki means universal life force energy and is available to all. The word derives from Rei, which means spirit or soul, and Ki, which means energy. The practice allows universal energy to flow through the Reiki practitioner to the person seeking treatment. Reiki touch points align with the chakras, which are energy fields within the body. **Healing touch is done with the intention of allowing for Spirit.**

Reiki formalizes the healing touch practice and provides a method for approaching healing energy work in a systematic way.

No ego is involved in the work because the Reiki healer doesn't control the flow of energy or the outcome. Reiki channels healing energy in the form needed by the person receiving it. Consequently, healing does not always mean recovery from an illness. Sometimes, the person receiving Reiki may need to surrender in order to die peacefully. In other situations, the person may require energetic support to complement traditional Western medical treatment or other healing modalities. Reiki's guiding principle is to serve the highest good.

For those not familiar with this healing method, keep an open mind. According to the Reiki Research Center, there are hospitals, medical clinics, and hospice programs where Reiki is offered as a standard part of care.

I initially sought Reiki training to unblock old patterns in my life. I met with a Master level Reiki instructor to learn how this tool worked. I found that it opened my creativity and my willingness to step into new dating relationships after the divorce. I received Maser level certification. The friend I mentioned earlier (in Chapter 1 on breathing) who lost his teenage son in a car wreck also got introduced to Reiki. At the time of his son's death, he already had a number of spiritual practices in place and enough resources on hand to prevent him from going down a destructive path of alcohol abuse. However, he found himself in such an intense state of grief that he remained at risk of giving up on life. The Reiki sessions provided him with an extra life preserver—something more to hold onto until he could navigate on his own again.

It's helpful to recognize when we need additional help, as well as the limits of our present learning. We may think we have our lives in a healthy, balanced place. But life keeps changing. What worked in the past may not work in the future. According to my friend,

Reiki—along with all the other tools he continued to practice—helped him reach a place of healing.

I practiced Reiki when my friend's husband, Tom, suffered a stroke. My friend asked people to perform Reiki on her husband—to assist in his healing and to support the work of the critical care nurses and physicians. Since I had received Master level Reiki training, I volunteered. Many people provided various healing modalities: sound therapy, shaman healing, aromatherapy, and other types of energy work—to name only a few.

As often is the case when we serve, we get more than we give. I came away from that experience with a greater appreciation for just being alive—for blue skies and sunshine, the ability to walk and go for a summer swim, and for the pleasure of sleeping in my own bed and eating a good meal. The doctors said they never expected Tom to recover. Because of the extent of his injuries, they thought he'd be a vegetable. I'm happy to report that he fully recovered and has taken an interest in Reiki. Both he and his wife use their talents to give back to the community in gratitude for all the love and help they received from friends, neighbors, family, nurses, doctors, physical therapists, and nontraditional healers. Miracles do happen! And those miracles may include some aspects of healing knowledge that Western medicine has not yet fully grasped.

Acupuncture

Traditional Chinese medicine includes the use of acupuncture for treating numerous health ailments. When I was experiencing premenopausal symptoms—waking up at night, night sweats, and irritability—two women friends recommended a local acupuncturist. I was hesitant to try it because the thought of needles isn't appealing to me. But the acupuncturist process turned out to be very relaxing. The needles are so small that they can hardly be felt and, meanwhile, I had an hour of lying still while listening to pleasant music. The tiny needles stimulate acupuncture points to correct imbalances in the flow of energy. After going through about five treatments, my night sweats disappeared. I have not experienced them since. I know other people who have used acupuncture for various health ailments. With Chinese medicine, other contributing health factors—such as eating, drinking, exercise, and sleep habits—are taken into account during treatment.

Loving Touch

Anytime we cradle a baby, hold hands, or hug a child, we are transferring healing energy through our love touch. Patting someone's shoulder, soulful hugs with friends who are hurting, and tender kisses with our partner connect us in a deeply healing way. Holding the hand of an elderly patient in a nursing home or greeting others with a genuine, warm handshake or friendly hug is an act of healing.

When my friend learned that his teenage son had died, I held his hand. In that moment, that was all I had to offer. I didn't have any words for such grief. Later, I took long walks with his wife and just listened. Sometimes simple acts are the most helpful. We can't take away someone's suffering. We can, however, let people know we care and give them a safe place to share their feelings and thoughts. Having someone to physically lean on during tough times really does help. Think about the situations where someone placed a hand on your arm, tenderly gripped your hand, or allowed you to cry on his or her shoulder. These small gestures can make a world of difference.

The same is also true when we practice loving sexual touch with our intimate life partners. Loving touch involves compassion, understanding, and respect. When you let someone into your physical space, trust and safety are absolutely essential. For such touch to be healing, it helps to view this energetic and physical exchange as a sacred act. For me, a long-term commitment to the relationship is also a necessary element. I believe such touch is an exchange on a soul level. As such, it isn't something to be entered into lightly or casually.

For nonsexual loving touch, we can practice hugging our friends, partners, elderly parents, relatives, and children. Having an animal to pet is another way to exchange positive healing energy through touch. When we kiss a baby's cheek, we also transfer positive energy. Touch of this kind is a form of unconditional love. **Ultimately, love is the basis for true inner healing.**

Smell

Smell is one of our strongest memory receptors. Certain smells can propel us back to childhood memories in an instant. Sage, nutmeg, or cinnamon scents may bring recollections of special holiday meals; a lit pipe or baked pie may remind you of a grandparent's home; and lilac or jasmine smells may remind you of a youthful stroll through a favorite garden spot. Smells easily transport us to another place and time stored in our memory (a wonderful scene in the movie *Harold and Maude* demonstrates this capacity of smell to mentally transport us). Unpleasant memories also get associated with smells. The smell of beer used to conjure up negative memories for me. Married now to a German who enjoys brewed beer, I no longer have the same associations with those smells. Pay attention to which smells evoke happy memories and which smells bother you. **If there's a strong emotional response, there may be a link to an important story from your past.** Smells can be useful in both healing emotional wounds and promoting spiritual wellness.

Aromatherapy

Recognizing which smells elicit feelings of peace, calm, and joy means that we can apply our sense of smell as a healing tool. Essential oils, scented candles, floral sachets, flowers, incense sticks, scented lotions, shampoo, and soaps can all be used to your benefit. You can apply a pleasant scent to your home, car, bath, or body. Lotions that smell good, for instance, may help you appreciate your body.

Certain smells have attributes typically associated with them. For instance, peppermint and citrus smells are used to energize, lavender to relax, and patchouli to evoke passion. Some faith traditions use burning sage or sandalwood to enhance a meditative state. What pleases the senses varies person to person. It's useful to learn which smells boost your mood. Recognizing that some odors may be putting your health at risk is crucial. If we're frequently around pollution, we begin not to notice the unpleasant smells until we leave the area for a time and then return. That can certainly be the case if you live in a city or near a factory for many years. It may take a vacation to a less polluted location for you to even notice the effect of car exhaust fumes and various manufacturing fumes that exist throughout the country.

Nontraditional healing methods, such as massage and aromatherapy, frequently use essential oils from plants. These oils are applied for ailments such as headaches, sinus problems, digestive troubles, arthritis, swollen feet, and other common physical complaints. When my friend Tom was in physical rehabilitation after his stroke, he asked for coconut smells. He said it reminded him of the beach and rubbing suntan oil on his wife's arms and legs.

Experiment with scents to find those that aid your health and wellness. If you can afford them, the benefits received from herbal soaps, essential oils, herbal shampoos, and herbal body lotions are worth the slightly higher price.

Taste

People consider taste only when it comes to planning their meals. But in most cultures, it's understood that certain herbs, spices, and foods contain healing properties. For centuries, Ayurveda (a traditional healing system that originated in India) and Traditional Oriental Medicine (which incorporates Chinese, Japanese, and Korean medicine) integrate food, minerals, and herbal remedies into their healing modalities.

According to *Natural Health and News*, basil, cayenne, cinnamon, garlic, ginger, oregano, turmeric and numerous other spices have beneficial healing properties. I remember when my daughters were younger and teething. I had read that clove had numbing properties when applied to the gums. I also recall my grandfather eating garlic as a daily illness preventive. When we learn which ingredients improve our health, alleviate allergies, and strengthen our immune system, we can use taste as an excellent tool for enhancing our health.

When we feel physically healthy, it's easier to face challenges in our day. If we're tired, stressed, and pumped full of caffeine and sugar, we react in much the same manner as young children who grow irritable with lack of sleep and an overload of sugar. Our bodies react—negatively or positively—according to the food we ingest.

There are many books devoted to the healing properties of herbs and the health benefits of organic, local whole foods. What you put in your body influences everything else. Take some time to explore how your body and mood react to certain foods and beverages and learn what your body needs for good health.

Pharmaceutical companies spend billions to discover which plants contain healing properties so that pills can be made and sold. If we spent as much money and time learning how native plants and natural foods benefit our healing, we might not require so many pills. **We might not need a cure for cancer and other health ailments if we understood better how to prevent these diseases.**

Fasting

Spiritual, religious, and health practices often include fasting for a set period of time. In a spiritual or religious context, it's a way to connect with Spirit. For example, in the Jewish tradition, Yom Kippur is considered the holiest day of the year and includes a sundown-to-sundown fast accompanied with prayer. In American Indian ceremonies, participants may fast for much longer periods while praying. A fast can also cleanse our bodies of built-up toxins. Even if your eating habits are healthy, a fast can bring greater mindfulness and appreciation of the food you consume. When I fast, I usually allow myself liquids such as water, tea, or juice. To date, I have not fasted for more than 48 hours.

I underwent my first fast with someone I was dating who had experience with fasting; he stayed with me from Friday night to Sunday dinnertime, the period of the fast. Given the amount of caffeine stored in my body, it's not surprising that the experience was unpleasant. I felt shaky and miserable. Fortunately, by the end of the fast, I became invigorated. Food never tasted so wonderful when it was finally time to sit down and enjoy a meal. Other friends have undergone three- and four-day fasts with no liquids while dancing in sacred ceremonies. Another friend fasts once a week, for 24 hours, as a health practice. As with any health practice, it's wise to check with a medical expert or health professional regarding the safety of a fast with your present health conditions.

For me, the absence of food and water served as a powerful reminder of our dependence on Mother Earth for our most vital needs. We are less likely to take food and water for granted when we have gone a period of time without them. It's also easier to identify with the suffering caused from starvation and malnutrition when we have experienced hunger pangs. We might also more readily recognize the sacrifice of animals when we go awhile without meat. As a spiritual practice, there's much to learn from the absence of food, when you are privileged enough to have that choice.

Energetic Impact

After spending time in Colorado for Native American ceremonies, I had a vivid dream about cows. They were gazing at me with huge brown eyes, a long row of them hung from a conveyor belt with their legs cut off. I had another similar dream regarding turkeys, all crammed into a huge warehouse building, hanging upside down by their legs. My developing compassion for animals made it difficult for me to gobble down my food without concern to what I was eating or how that animal had been treated before it found its way to my plate. The energy of the animal may have communicated with me because my dreams came after meals of those particular foods. It could also be that my own sense of ethics was trying to get my attention.

How food is prepared can also affect us. I ordered a burrito once from a restaurant where the workers were visibly stressed and angry because of a large lunchtime crowd and too few employees to meet the demand. After I ate, I got a headache. I had not been feeling stressed. I also had ordered my food to go and ate elsewhere. But I believe my body felt the negative energy put into the food. On the other hand, food prepared by a loving parent when a child is ill or by a partner on special occasions brings comfort. Such foods lift our spirits.

Most people want to make good decisions based on their spiritual or religious value systems. But sometimes we get so busy that we don't take action on those beliefs. Food is one area where eating quickly because of schedule demands or purchasing meat products from mistreated animals because of economic concerns is common. For instance, I know that nonrecyclable materials can be destructive for the environment. Yet, when I purchase items, I don't always consider this factor. Sometimes I forget while eating that the animals were factory farmed with no regard for humane treatment. I may also forget that my paper napkin, to-go box, and paper plate are from a tree that once was once part of a beautiful forest. Because I live in an urban setting, sometimes I may even forget that there are beautiful forests.

Yet, it's absolutely vital that what we eat and how we eat gets integrated into our spiritual practice. Everything affects everything else. You can't separate your use of paper from the forest that no longer exists in your town or city. Trees provide shelter for animals, cooling shade during intense heat, roots for soil irrigation, oxygen for breathing, and numerous other benefits that we quickly forget when we don't pay attention to those teachings. Your health and the health of your children are affected by the existence or nonexistence of trees. The planet's health is directly related to our survival. A sick environment makes for sick people. A healthy environment aids our overall health.

One solution to a healthier and happier life is to pay attention to your food selection and how it's prepared. I asked my daughters one Sunday what they would like to do that they considered spiritual. I was surprised when they both selected cooking. We got a recipe, a list of ingredients, cooked the food, and then shared in eating it. We also discussed what would make the cooking spiritual. Their answer: cooking with love. That afternoon activity brought us all immense joy. We enjoyed the new adventure, the group planning, the preparing and sharing of the meal.

Food prepared with love nourishes those who prepare it and those who consume it. When I prepare meals as a chore, it tastes different than when I cook a special meal for someone I love. If I'm feeling angry while eating, I barely taste my food. Think about your favorite childhood foods. Ice cream, cinnamon toast, and fresh blueberries remind me of time with my grandmother. When I am feeling silly, happy, or joyful, those foods come to mind. It's important that what you eat lifts your spirits and brings you healthy doses of happiness. We can also give thanks for the animals, plants, sunshine, rain, and many hands that made our meal possible.

Sense Questions to Explore:
- What visuals lift my mood?
- How can I add healthy touch to my life?
- What smells bring me pleasure?
- What could I do differently to make food consumption a spiritual practice?

Exercise: Putting Your Senses to Use

For the next week, pay extra attention to the sights and smells in your environment. What visuals do you want to add or remove? Write down the smells you observe in your home, workplace, and neighborhood. Notice the foods you eat for breakfast, lunch, and dinner. Keep track of those food sources. Are they local, organic, factory-farmed? How is the food prepared? Are you receiving or giving hugs? Do you have an animal to pet or monthly massage appointment? Choose three things you can do to improve your body awareness or sense environment.

CHAPTER 4

SPIRIT: Finding Inner Peace

*"Few find inner peace but this is not because they try and fail,
it is because they do not try."*
—**Peace Pilgrim**

We put so much pressure on ourselves—and allow other people to put enormous pressure on us—that we risk heart attacks, high blood pressure, and strokes. We pick up a daily list of worries, we rush, we honk horns, and we yell at each other. To get in touch with your life, your spirit, and your soul, you'll need to slow down enough to realize what exists when you step off a crazed autopilot. You need time to ask and answer the questions presented by your life: Why are you stressed? Is stress necessary? Does worry help you find solutions or cause confusion and chaos? It's not easy to make healthy decisions when your life is spinning out of control. You first have to move away from the force of the suction and get out of the mental churning.

It can be a huge challenge in our culture to do nothing for an hour, a day, a weekend, or a week. Yet, it may take an entire day just to let go of our mind chatter, open up to empty space, and detoxify from all the junk taking up so much room in our minds and bodies. Once you release all that internal clutter, you have an opportunity to hear what Spirit has to say.

Even if your life is relatively calm, allotting peaceful time for inner reflection and soul connection can keep you on target with your life purpose and re-energize you for the work ahead. If you don't take time to replenish your own spirit, you won't have anything of value to offer anyone else. As they tell parents on the airplane: In the event of an emergency, put your own air mask on first. **Making spiritual growth a priority in your life benefits not only you but also everyone you come into contact with.**

Retreats

One way to be intentional about setting aside time for Spirit is to attend a retreat. It's far too easy in our daily lives to get distracted and pulled into the crisis du jour (of the day). On a retreat, you can avoid telephone calls, emails, Facebook, text messaging, and continual interruptions from the outside world. A retreat allows you to connect with your authentic self when not pushed or influenced by outside factors. With only your own thoughts and an expanse of time to dwell in—unhurried and without an agenda—you can be present to whatever shows up in the moment.

There are excellent reasons for attending retreats. People go on retreats to heal grief from a loss. Some people attend as a religious or spiritual commitment. Other people go for periods of creative renewal or to get clarity on a troubling problem or difficult challenge. Sometimes a retreat is simply a means of nurturing self-care. I've attended many types of retreats for various purposes. I've gone on solo retreats to focus on my writing, nature retreats and Vision Quests to commune with Spirit, group meditation retreats to learn skills and allot a block of time for meditation, women drumming retreats to creatively and spiritually connect with friends, and women circle group retreats to participate in meaningful rituals. All of these retreats have proven beneficial.

Solo Retreats

Planning a solo retreat presents a unique occasion to forge out time for your innermost needs. How often do we ask ourselves what we really need and then take time to put that plan in place? Self-care and spiritual growth are not selfish. They help you become more fully the person you want to be out in the world—whether your world is family, work, creative pursuits, community leadership, care of others, retirement, or some combination thereof. Whatever role you play or mask you wear in your daily life, a retreat allows you to look within, strip always the labels, and discover what replenishes your spirit.

A retreat center is a good place to start. The advantage of an established center is that it may provide eating facilities, safety, and peaceful surroundings. Many centers offer private quarters away from group activities. Religious retreat centers don't always require an affiliation with their faith. If you prefer something more informal, you can also set up your own solo retreat with a camping tent at a state park or by renting a cabin or reserving a room at a bed and breakfast. Your retreat might last a day, a weekend, or a week or more, depending on your needs and circumstances. It can be as simple as a day spent at a nearby park. Or you might travel a great distance for a weeklong retreat at a beachside resort, religious hermitage, or artist colony.

One life lesson I've learned is that a solo retreat doesn't mean you should be without support. A facility that includes meal options can make life a lot easier. Additionally, be sure to let someone know where you're going. Ask for their care while you're gone, whether it's sending you prayers or bringing in your mail.

Once on a solo retreat, I decided to undertake a solitary faith quest. To me, a faith quest meant staying out in nature alone overnight. I didn't have any Native American teachings (or outdoor survival skills), and I hadn't discussed my plan with anyone. I was staying at a retreat lodge center surrounded by 400 acres of beautiful wooded lands. I went out walking one afternoon and came upon a meadow where I saw a deer standing along the edge of the woods. I took it as a sign. I opted not to return to my lodge room. Instead, I planned to stay right where I was all night. It was a warm spring day, and I was dressed in shorts and a T-shirt.

As evening fell, I sat and gazed at lightning bugs flickering across the meadow. I noticed storm clouds in the distance and watched as they rolled in. The sky grew darker, and the air turned brisk and chilly. The retreat lodge was in southeastern Indiana, and there had been recent severe tornadoes in the area. The weather soon grew more and more threatening; I started shivering with cold. Fierce thunder and lightning came closer as it began to storm. At one point, when the lightening was near, I threw my room and car keys a short distance away, fearing that any metal I was holding might be the cause of my death. As the storm hit hard overhead, I mentally said goodbye to loved ones and regretted that I hadn't told anyone what I was doing. It's difficult to describe the state of fear that gripped me. I began praying. Then, I heard an American Indian song that I'd heard only once before. I also envisioned strong women from my Goddess Circle, and I formed a circle of safety around myself—with sticks and focused imagination. I waited until the worst of the storm had passed and then I left, jogging back to the retreat lodge and vowing never to do anything like that again.

Although I made it through that retreat unharmed, it was a reminder to touch base with people I love before wandering off and to plan ahead so that the experience is not life endangering. On a solo retreat, bring along the love of all who care for you. Whatever your spiritual, religious, or scientific beliefs, humans don't exist in a vacuum. Similarly, what you bring back from your retreat is your contribution to the community. Once during a Vision Quest in Colorado, I told a friend that I was concerned about my time away from my daughters. The friend reminded me that I was on the Vision Quest for my daughters. Everything we learn ripples back out to our friends, family, neighbors, and workplaces. (Chapter 7 discusses my Vision Quest and the meaningful role your spiritual community can play in any retreat). As we grow in spiritual depth and wisdom, the greater whole benefits. We are like a vast field of flowers, each peaceful blossom adding beauty to the landscape.

Nature Retreats

A nature retreat connects you with Mother Earth. You can observe the vibrating buzz of cicadas, the smooth glide of a soaring hawk, the rapid movements of a fast-flowing river, the sturdiness of mountains, the majesty of trees, and the ever-present energy of Spirit. You can ask what you might learn from the trees, creatures, and plants in the natural environment. Animals offer us many useful lessons. **When you notice an animal, you can ask what the animal wants to teach you.**

Deer hold meaning in my life. While on a retreat in Northern Indiana, I was walking near some trees on the outskirts of a large farm field and saw a flash of white. I stood still, wondering if I'd seen a dog's tail. Then I noticed three deer nearby. When they galloped off, I followed their trail down to a river that I hadn't known was there. The river eventually led to a school. On the walk back, I saw the deer again. On my Vision Quest in Colorado, a mule deer walked slowly past. On a third retreat, near the border of Kentucky, I happened upon an outdoor labyrinth and discovered a fawn sleeping in one of the paths (Chapter 2 discusses labyrinths and the fawn discovery). The deer remind me, in the Buddhist tradition, of a gentle spirit. Deer give me permission to walk a quiet, peaceful path even in a world preoccupied with violence, skepticism, and anger. My path is the only one I walk. I can't walk for others. As I walk my path, the deer of compassion accompanies me. I don't ever need to deny the gentle side of my character just because someone else walks a different path or someone else doesn't understand or appreciate my gifts. I don't need to become an ox, fox, or tiger. **I am complete as I am. I don't have to become something I'm not.**

On a nature retreat, seek out guidance for your life. Follow the path that calls. When you're in tune with nature, you become more aware of your place in the larger world. You begin to notice the way leaves shimmer in the breeze and the way sunlight sparkles across the water. Your body slows down and gets into a different rhythm. You may experience moments of intense boredom and loneliness or moments of insight and joy. Even the loneliness and boredom can teach you about your life. You can ask questions, reflect upon the answers, and listen for guidance from the natural world. **Spirit will bring what you need.**

Group Retreats

If you want a retreat experience but also desire some structure and interaction with others, a group retreat may meet your needs.

An advantage of this type of retreat is the chance to meet people with similar interests. Another plus is the opportunity to learn from those who are more advanced in specific practice areas. For instance, a Buddhist retreat may include teachings on Buddhist principles and meditation techniques. A yoga retreat likely has an experienced instructor who offers his or her skills. The facilities, food, and activities are already established for group retreats, leaving you free to simply attend and absorb the experience.

The duration of group retreats varies, some last a day and others extend over a weekend. While most people who work can't attend lengthy retreats, there are some that go for weeks or months. Restrictions for group retreats vary according to their purpose. Some are open to both men and women, and others are intended exclusively for one gender group. Retreats exist for all sorts of religious, spiritual, and self-growth aims. They may focus on creative expression, meditation, silence, body movement, ancestral chants, relaxation, nature, or alternative health practices—to namely only a few possible areas of exploration. Workplaces and religious communities may also offer retreats. Individuals involved in public service, teaching, creative endeavors, spiritual work, health care professions, business enterprises, and healing fields need ways to come together for support and rejuvenation.

My first group retreat was a writing retreat. I attended a Quaker retreat with guest writers who gave lectures and workshops. This retreat was designed to provide inspiration, networking, and guidance for writers. Since then, I've attended women's drumming retreats, yoga intensives, Buddhist meditation retreats, Goddess Circle retreats, and Wisdom Circle retreats. The drumming retreat incorporated elements of dance and song, along with basic drumming instructions. Shared meals and group activities helped me meet new people and strengthen existing friendships. The yoga intensive provided small group discussion activities, lectures, and yoga instruction.

My meditation retreats, although done in a group, were primarily focused on silent meditation and vegetarian meals that we ate in silence. The retreat took place with my sangha community and followed a structured meditation schedule. The gathering was designed to bolster and support each individual's meditation practice. For instance, if I only meditate in the privacy of my home, I might not be self-motivated enough to get up at 5 a.m. or to meditate for an hour. But at a retreat, I can get into the habit of meditating for longer periods.

My Goddess Circle and Wisdom Circle retreats served my need to connect with women on similar spiritual paths. At these retreats, I spent enjoyable time with women friends as we discussed ways in which our spirituality could assist with current life challenges. The women who attended these retreats set an informal, loose agenda. We shared our personal stories, hopes, and fears in a safe space and incorporated meals, rituals, and enjoyable fun activities into the retreat experience.

Both formalized teachings and informal community activities provide useful opportunities for growth. At a group retreat, you can try things you might never explore on your own. You may chant as the sun rises or dance to a drumbeat under a moonlit sky. The positive group energy adds to the overall experience. A group retreat can also be as simple as getting together with friends to discuss a spiritual book or fine-tune a spiritual practice while staying at a cabin or rented house. If the friends share a common vision and spiritual purpose, the retreat will provide an informal way to further group learning, development, and strength. Such a retreat can be a reminder of your values and life purpose and serve as inspiration for when members are no longer on the retreat.

Take a Time Out

Even if you can't attend a solo or group retreat, practice deep relaxation as a way to connect with Spirit. For instance, you can try sitting outside in the sun while listening to birds chirping or neighborhood children laughing. Bask in the scent of flowers and trees. Discover what's possible when you take time to play, sing, dance, or lounge in the park on a sunny day. Sit comfortably or walk patiently and simply observe the world around you for 20 minutes. **Just relax.** No cell phones, reading, laptops, talking, or television. Walk or sit, and notice life go past. Watch clouds floating across the sky or listen to geese honking overhead.

The ability to relax—mentally, emotionally, and physically— takes practice. But relaxation is key to helping you process angry, stressed, and obsessive thoughts. If you can't solve your problems, you can at least take some time to nurture yourself. Depending on what's tugging at your mind and churning your emotions, you may have to sit with the issue for a while. But you'd be surprised how watching the sky for brief periods improves your outlook.

Your Dream Terrain

There are infinite levels of knowing. The dream landscape presents a level below conscious awareness. Paying attention to your dreams can give you insights that you might miss during your hectic day. For instance, when I was working excessive hours at a law job, I had a dream that I drove to work and parked my car in the parking garage, and the whole garage collapsed. At the time, my job was taking a toll on my physical and emotional health. The dream was a way to communicate those concerns. **Symbols go deeper than language and verbal expression.** They represent what's important to you and may also show you what in your life needs to change.

Different methods can assist you in interpreting your dream symbols. I often refer to a book with dream symbols by a woman from the Chippewa tribe. She learned from an elder and passed along those insights. She believes that water represents spiritual elements, a car represents your body and physical health, and hair represents your thoughts. So, a dream about a boat traveling across the ocean, for example, might give you information about your spiritual path. With such a dream, you could examine the type of boat (is it a luxury liner, rowboat, or some other water craft), the water conditions (are the waves rough or calm), and the passengers on the boat with you (are you alone or with a crowd). You could ask what the dream is trying to communicate and journal about those visions and insights.

I also refer to Ted Andrews' book, *Animal Speak*. Although his book isn't about dream symbols, it does discuss what different animals represent for us. If I dream about a dolphin or hawk, for instance, I may read his book and learn that dolphins are intelligent, playful creatures, and hawks carry spiritual messages. I can then discern additional dream interpretations from those attributes. When I need emotional strength, a bear or black panther may appear in my dream landscape. A unicorn and dragonflies have appeared during times of creativity. Animals are wonderful dream symbols to explore.

Other people use psychology-based interpretations or mythological archetypes to discover the meanings behind common dream symbols. At a dream workshop I attended, the instructor used ancient archetypes to explain the roles played out in our dream landscape and in our lives. For instance, he would examine common attributes, such as love (Aphrodite), strength (Artemis) and wisdom (Sophia), to find recurring themes. Significantly, he emphasized that **all dreams come in the service of healing and wholeness**.

Your dreams symbols don't need to be overly complicated or psychologically analyzed in order to provide useful guidance. You can examine your dreams and decide what the animals, people, or events mean for you. Try keeping a dream journal. Useful insights can be gained through this process.

People who have died may also show up in dreams offering direction for your life or greater understanding of a situation. We are connected on many levels to everything that surrounds us. It's not surprising that connections with people close to us occasionally cross over into our dreams, especially during emotionally intense states. I've had a dream where someone I knew had cancer; that person later verified that he had received news of a cancer diagnosis. I've had dreams of people who have passed on and are worried about their children or are passing along some bit of information. It's rare for me, but these types of dreams do occur. Some people may experience these sorts of dreams more often.

Dreams function in a variety of ways. Some dreams are simply fear-based. Some dreams help process problems. Some represent hopes and desires. Some are wake-up calls for taking a different course of action or following a new life direction. And some are intuitive, premonition dreams.

Dreams offer helpful suggestions of what to let go of and what to add each day. If I dream that my child has died, I make a conscious effort to appreciate more fully our time together. If I dream I'm traveling on a raft floating down a river and seeing beautiful scenery pass along the way, after having a dream where the parking garage at work collapses, I reaffirm to myself that I need to take steps to pursue alternative career paths. The subconscious offers input beyond the rational. I had a dream once where someone told me that I needed more joyful entries in the last chapters of my life book. By allowing time for my writing and embarking on enjoyable nature hikes and family vacations, I can turn that dream advice into a reality for my life. **Dream interpretations are useful when they support what you already know in your heart to be true.**

A Daily Journal

By writing in a daily journal, you bring to light your habitual patterns and your creative possibilities for change. Journal writing releases the internal garbage taking up space in your mind by giving you an outlet. With journaling, you explore the hidden roots of who you are. You can use a page or three pages to vent and then go deeper by examining your heartfelt desires. As mentioned, you can use the journal to record dreams. You can also use a journal to spontaneously write whatever comes to mind. **Such writing permits you to fully access your hopes and fears.**

With journal writing, you begin to make helpful observations about your life. Julia Cameron in *The Artist's Way* is a strong proponent of journal writing as a means for tapping into your creative potential. Another interesting writing method that my husband has used is to switch hands while writing in order to access childhood reflections. Your adult self writes as normal. But your child writes with your nondominant other hand. You can ask and answer questions of yourself in this way.

Pay attention to what you have to say to yourself. Without self-censorship, you can learn where you want to head on your life journey. Change happens. **You need only listen to the inner voice hidden deep in your heart.** If your daily mind is preoccupied with the bustle of job, family, and schedules, your journal writing can bring out what needs healing and attention. The upside is that you don't have to vent all your worries, fears, and anger onto other people. And if you do need to discuss something, you can then do so in a calmer state of mind.

Shamanism

Shamans travel the Spirit worlds. They may meet animal helpers and spirit guides to retrieve healing wisdom. There is much that modern science can't explain. When you allow all possibilities for healing to enter your life, some paths that reveal themselves may be unfamiliar. They may also be scary and not seem "rational." To travel the unknown requires bravery. If you keep your heart and mind open, you may discover wonderful new spiritual avenues that work for you.

In my initial experience with shamanism, an acquaintance leading a group session asked us to partner with someone, lie down, and relax. She led the group on a guided meditation, and I was her partner. I felt skeptical of the whole process and not close friends with this particular person. I had no set expectations—and quite a bit of impatience. I assumed the session would merely provide some needed relaxation time. I was lying down with my eyes closed, listening to the guided meditation, and slowly relaxing. The person leading the session was leaning over me.

Suddenly, I saw my father holding me as an infant. I could feel his love for me. I have no idea how my brain could possibly retrieve such a distant memory, but it did. I felt a heavy burden being lifted from my shoulders and, more importantly, from my heart. When the session ended and we opened our eyes, I remained silent. The person who led the meditation said she saw a brown color lifting away from my forehead area, and it looked like a releasing of some heaviness. I didn't share my personal experience. I didn't think anyone would believe me. I was so surprised by the turn of events and not sure how to process my emotions. Because my father had left when I was 4, I had always assumed he didn't love me. I never told anyone that I carried that burden, and I still haven't told the group facilitator (or anyone from that group) the incredible gift I received that evening.

Shortly after this shamanism session, I was at a family gathering for the holidays. Out of nowhere, my aunt began telling me how my father used to hold me and dress me as a baby and how unusual that behavior was for a man during the early 1960s. I had not asked my aunt about my biological father, and I had not mentioned the shamanism session to anyone. She volunteered that information out of the blue. For some reason, Spirit wanted me to understand on a very deep level that the information I had received was true. My aunt's story confirmed that my experience in the shamanism session was real; I had not simply imagined it. I had received what I needed in the spirit of healing. My father had loved me.

Later, the women who led the shamanism session recommended a series of peace and community healing shamanism workshops. A nationally recognized shaman led these workshops. His teachings involved group drumming, chanting, rattles, whistles, safe space, journeying, and a community intention for prayers, healing, and guidance from Spirit.

In one of the sessions, I had another experience that went beyond rational explanation. During a group drumming, we formed two circles. Some of us remained in the inner circle, and others were in the outer circle. I was on the inside, listening to the drums and rattles. At some point, we were asked to go to someone in the outer circle who needed healing energy. I went directly to a woman behind me and hugged her. As I did so, the word "mom" popped into my head. My intent was just to extend loving energy to her. But when I returned back to the inner circle, I felt an intense chill, as though something significant had taken place. I wasn't sure what had happened. When I talked to her later, I learned that the woman's daughter had died. She told me the story of her daughter's death. I listened. I believe her daughter had been there briefly with her mom to offer healing.

We share moments of healing with each other all the time, even though we may not know exactly how or why these healings happen. If someone had told me earlier of the incidents above, I never would have believed it. When I first heard the word shamanism, my immediate reaction was disbelief. **All I can say is that we learn as we go.** We may not believe something until it happens to us and becomes part of our personal experience.

Shamanism allows for the possibility of realms beyond current understanding. It creates a space where we can receive healing and offer healing to others. Like most spiritual healing methods, shamanism accesses deeper levels of consciousness.

Teachings From Death

Many traditions encourage the contemplation of impermanence. Someday we will die. Our friends, family, and loved ones also will die. This news isn't meant to be depressing. On the contrary, fully accepting this reality teaches you to appreciate your life and your time with those you love.

When my children were young and I drove them both to school, our mornings were often chaotic and frustrating. It seemed we were always rushing to get ready and trying not to be late. But I reminded myself, as they scurried out of the car and headed toward the school, that this might be the last time I saw them. I always gave them a hug, told them I loved them, and then watched as they joined the animated throng of children rushing into the building. Tomorrow isn't guaranteed for anyone. I remember hearing the story of a woman who lost her husband, saying to her young children, "We had no worries before." **Death reminds us how precious, fragile, and tender this life truly is.**

When I was around 5, an Italian family baby-sat me. In addition to the parents, there were four children—three boys and one girl. They had a gigantic yard with a merry-go-round, a pool, and pear trees that lined the far back section. Even better, their house was right next door to my grandparents. All the boisterous activity with hide-and-seek games and running around outside with the other neighborhood kids created a childhood paradise. One week, they went on a family vacation and the dad drove his pickup truck, which had a camper on back. While driving home, the dad fell asleep at the wheel, causing an accident. He and two of the children—the girl and the youngest boy—were killed.

I listened as my grandmother relayed this tragic news. Two of my playmates and their dad had died. I wouldn't be going to their house anymore. Even though I can vividly recall my grandmother telling me this information, I can't recall now what emotional affect their deaths had on me. I have many memories associated with this time, including a visit to the doctor when I fell on a cola bottle at their house, eating cauliflower for the first time, and thinking I was too big for a high chair—the only seat they had available for me. Still, I can't remember how I felt about these deaths. I imagine my reaction was similar to hearing horrific news about strange events in faraway places. We recognize that the news is true but, on some level, we can't fully grasp that such a thing has really happened. Nevertheless, I still carry this story close to my heart today. An entire family had their lives drastically altered in one brief instant. **There are no guarantees that any of us will be here tomorrow.**

When people close to us die or we face death ourselves, our perspective on things can shift. My aunt and uncle lost their son, Little Ray, to leukemia. I don't have memories regarding the details of my cousin's death because I was so young and he was 2 ½ years younger than I. But my uncle shared the story with me years later.

In high school, Uncle Raymond had been a state boxing champion in Michigan. He then joined the military and served in Vietnam. His lifestyle was typical for a good-looking, popular young man coming of age during the '60s. When he returned to the States and got married, he and his wife tried to have children. She suffered a number of miscarriages. Eventually, they had a baby boy that they named after my uncle. That child had leukemia and died young. When Little Ray was dying, he told his parents not to worry, that he had seen Jesus and Jesus told him it was going to be OK.

In the intensity of their grief, my aunt and uncle decided to commit suicide. Ray was stationed out west at the time. He and his wife got in their car with the intent of driving to a mountain area and jointly committing suicide. My uncle says that while they were driving, he suddenly saw the sky open to reveal a beautiful and dazzling sunlit expanse. He asked his wife if she saw it too, and she said, *yes.* He pulled off the road and into a parking lot. When they knocked on the door of a nearby building, a woman immediately answered and said that she knew they were coming because she had been praying and saw it in a vision. The building was a church. This radically life-altering experience resulted in my uncle becoming an ordained minister. He has since dedicated his life to assisting veterans and spreading God's joy.

It wasn't until I was in high school that I next encountered the loss of people I knew. Two classmates died. One boy hung himself, and the other boy died from a gunshot wound during a hunting trip. Students were not given enough information to know if the hunting trip incident was accidental or intentional. For those of us who were friends with that student, we knew he drank a lot of alcohol and experimented with drugs. We concluded, rightly or wrongly, that it was suicide.

During the early 1980s, high schools didn't hold school assembly meetings or counseling sessions for students the way they might do today when a student dies. When I heard the news from friends about the boy who died on the hunting trip, I felt like I was watching the world through a fishbowl: Everything appeared slightly distorted but continued on as normal. Students processed this event in the way youth tend to do when left to their own methods: We talked among ourselves and found our own coping mechanisms, often involving alcohol. I remember so many classmates who just felt incredibly lost during high school because their home lives were in shambles or due to their own addictions and excessive use of harmful substances.

As a young adult, I lost three males cousins—two by what appeared to be accidental drug overdoses while drinking and one in an automobile accident. An uncle, the father of one of my cousins, died in his mid-50s from a heart attack a year or so after his son's death. I believe his heart was broken; unfortunately, he coped with his grief through alcohol and cigarettes. As mentioned earlier, my own father died in an alcohol-related driving accident. More recently,

I lost my high school best friend to a form of leukemia. This longtime friend was in her 40s; she was married to a wonderful man and was the mother of three beautiful daughters. Now, in midlife, my experiences with death also involve friends who are losing their parents.

It's said that we come to Spirit with wounds as big as God. All these deaths have propelled me along a path that looks at why some people are able to navigate through suffering in a healthy way and others are not. It has become my lifelong mission to find healing tools to help people make it through hardships. I also try to foster daily gratitude for friends and family who are here. I appreciate time with my husband and daughters. I remind myself (and my daughters) of the importance of following dreams. I am intentional about having more moments of joy and gratitude.

A friend from work who regularly attended church, prayed, and read religious texts said that years ago when her son died, she felt like she didn't have a single prayer left in her. She still attended church, but she was angrily questioning why God took her child and what kind of God would take a child. In describing her life at that time, she said it felt like she was walking through tar—nothing that worked before was helping answer her questions or heal her grief. Like many couples that face intense grief, she and her husband also went through a divorce. As my friend acknowledges today, she came out the other side of that struggle stronger. She learned, for her, that it is not about what "you" want. After her son died, she was at home one day and prayer came back, only now the prayer was from a deeper place. She has since remarried, raised grandchildren, and found inner peace. She feels joyful and blessed. She believes her purpose in life is to help others feel joyful. Her life is focused on offering kind words, showing compassion toward others, and expressing gratitude. She embodies strength of Spirit. You can't shake her with ordinary concerns. She has been through too much hardship to let petty issues ruin her day.

These lessons aren't easy. Yet, death is an inescapable part of the life cycle. No one lives forever. Had each of us been raised in a culture where death was honored as a celebration of passing into the next level of being, we might not become as overwrought on hearing news of a death. In Western culture, we understand that death is a natural occurrence as people age, but we miss people who leave their physical bodies, and we feel devastated if they leave in what we perceive to be "before their time." I've heard it said that no one can say how long a flower should bloom or how long a life should last. However, we desperately want that beauty to last. I don't know the answers for healing in these situations. I can only offer up what has helped some people. **We all do the best we can to figure out the meaning and purpose of our lives.** With my father's death, I learned gratitude for time with my children and for the relationship I have with my daughters—something he had only briefly with me.

Not long ago, a close friend of mine from church, Norma Bradway, died of cancer. She had been an attorney who worked tirelessly for women's rights; many years ago, she fought for married women to have the legal right to obtain credit cards in their own names. Shortly before her death, I spent time at her bedside. She gave me a card that she had made with the word "hope" and a beautiful image of a woman surrounded by rainbow light. We talked briefly, and I could see what looked to me like a mask of death on her face. She was ready to die. A few days later when she died, I was walking through a wooded area. A large owl flew over my head, forcing me to look up. They sky was stunningly beautiful. I felt her spirit leaving like an exhaled breath of incredible bliss. I felt happy and immediately thought people should wear bright colors to her funeral and celebrate her passing. I missed her and I cried, but I felt such gratitude for her friendship and, for some reason, I felt peaceful about her passing rather than anguished. I haven't ever again experienced that sense of death as a beautiful expression of a soul moving on. I doubt I would have noticed or felt it at all had it been my child or a lover. But that one experience did open me to the possibility that death can feel joyful in some situations. I have enormous gratitude for the gifts I received from her friendship and the gifts I continue to receive from her. **As Chief Seattle wisely said, "There is no death, only a change of worlds."**

Contemplating our death or another person's death reminds us to prioritize, let go of old hurts, and tell people we love them. Staying aware of death encourages you to live more authentically, love more fully, and appreciate the people who are in your life.

Death Inventory:

- **If you had six months to live, or if your children or partner had six months to live, what would you do differently?**
- **If today were your last day, if saying goodbye to someone turned out to be the last time you saw that person, what would you say?**
- **What lessons did you miss in this lifetime?**
  - ➢ **How to forgive?**
  - ➢ **How to love?**
  - ➢ **How to acquire a deeper faith?**
- **What gifts have people offered you while you were here?**

- **If you died tomorrow, have you made amends to those you hurt?**
- **Did you fully appreciate your life?**
- **Is there something more you want to contribute before you die?**
- **Are you grateful for the people in your life?**

Prayer

It's said that in meditation we listen to Spirit, and in prayer we talk to Spirit. Even if you don't belong to an organized religion or follow any particular spiritual practices, prayer is an incredible tool when you need guidance, support, or comfort. **A heartfelt prayer doesn't require anything of you; yet, it gives you so much in return.**

There are infinite ways to pray. Prayer isn't limited to places of worship. It also doesn't require people to be down on their knees—although that's certainly one common approach. Think about all the ways people pray. They pray on airplanes, at gravesides, in hospitals, after a telephone call regarding bad news, in an emergency, during the birth of a child, a serious illness, marriage, separation, death of a spouse, before tests or important activities, after a loss, when worried about a friend or family member, and before going to sleep at night.

Some faiths ritualize prayers for certain events, such as before meals or during a religious service, and other religions, such as Islam, have prayer throughout the day. American Indian tribes use sweat lodges, sacred tobacco, ancestor stones, and a calling of the directions. Despite the myriad beneficial ways to pray, it helps to remember that prayer can be as simple as a whisper in your mind that says, "*Please help me.*" Prayer isn't a wish list like a letter to Santa Claus or a way to get what you want. It's communication from your heart and openness to what serves your highest good and the highest good for others— which may or may not be the answer you wanted. I know I've shed many tears over relationships and job situations that, in hindsight, were never in my best interest. Not getting that relationship or that job led me to better things that Spirit had in store for me.

When I'm experiencing extreme emotional turmoil over a situation and can't solve it myself, I write down the name of the person who is troubling me, ask for guidance, and then set the paper aside. To me, that is prayer. If I'm having difficulty, I sometimes pray to my deceased grandfather because I know he loved me very much. If I feel extreme stress at work, I may look out the window and offer up a prayer to the sky while asking for help with the situation. If I'm feeling sad and sitting on the riverbank, I may pray to the river. In a circle group with women friends, we may offer prayers to the Feminine Divine. At night before I sleep, I may pray to God. The words of the prayer or the deity named are not as important as sharing what's in your heart, seeking wisdom, and staying open for guidance. A prayer is your soul reaching out to the universe, angels, trees, sun, or God of your religious or spiritual beliefs. It's intimate, personal, and private. You don't have to worry about being misunderstood, embarrassed, or judged. You can disclose your innermost longings, fears, hopes, dreams, disappointments, mistakes, and sorrows. **You can release in your prayers whatever it is that you need to turn over to a higher source.**

If you've never prayed before, here is what works for me. I sit quietly and talk to someone I love that has died. I tell that person my sorrow or concern and ask him or her to watch over and guide me. My other favorite prayer method is to sit in nature and send out my prayers without any specific words. I take some deep breaths and, if I use words, I simply ask for guidance and help. Sometimes I find a quiet spot near a tree and meditate or simply cry. Your life can be a prayer. The job you perform each day, the way you raise your children, and the creative expressions you put out into the world can all be your prayers. As I mentioned in the beginning of the book, my writings also serve as my prayers. When your heart is open, you may discover many ways to pray.

Once after sitting quietly in a downtown church during my lunchtime work break, I noticed two men sitting on the church steps. As I descended the steps, one of the men asked me to pray with him. I shook my head no, thinking they were joking or making fun of me. I was also thinking, "I'm not a minister. I don't know how to pray." The man asked me again to pray with him, and he held out his hand. Both men appeared serious. I shrugged and walked over and took his hands. He closed his eyes, and so I shut my eyes. I was not using the word prayer for that exchange. I just held his hands, opened my heart, and let go mentally. When we opened our eyes, he smiled and thanked me. Incredibly, I felt like I was the one who had benefited. I felt happier in spirit as I walked away, thanking him. We never exchanged names or more than a few words, but somehow the intent and connection put a lighter beat to my steps for the rest of my day and, hopefully, did the same for him.

Prayers may also be in the form of songs or chants. A song or chant allows a prayer to go beyond our specific needs and into larger, universal themes of gratitude, love, and healing. Songs and chants in the form of prayers are used in Native American ceremonies, Goddess rituals, religious hymns, and Buddhist meditative chants, to name only a few. These rhythms can help us feel connected to Spirit. Praying in this way can be extremely powerful.

Explore the idea that prayer is more expansive and more meaningful than your current understanding of the word. If you're in an unfamiliar city, another country, at work, in a hospital, prison, or airport, you may not have access to candles, beads, bells, holy water, drums, singing bowls, pipes, fire, stones, an altar, a cross, or a sanctuary. If you're in a hurricane, on a plane, or in a traffic accident, prayer—whether for self or others—is a direct conversation from your heart to your god.

Know that prayers from deep within will bring you what you most need. **As Saint Francis of Assisi said, "Pray without ceasing; if necessary, use words."**

CHAPTER 5

DISCOVER YOUR PATH:
Embarking on the Journey

"Do not seek to follow in the footsteps of the ancient ones;
seek what they sought."
—Matsuo Bashō, Japanese poet (1644–1694)

A common spiritual saying is, "There are many paths up to the mountaintop." There are also many mountains. In other words, there are many truths, many religious and spiritual wisdom teachings, and many names for Spirit: Wankan Tanka, Creator, Goddess, Brahman, God, Allah, Yahweh, Baya, Vishnu, Oya, Enlightenment, Universal Energy, Supreme Truth, and All That Is, to cite only a few. If you travel the world, you'll find countless faiths: Hinduism, Islam, Buddhism, Christianity, Paganism, Judaism, Unitarian Universalism, Quaker, Sufism, Science of Mind, Baha´'i´, American Indian tribal beliefs, and various indigenous faiths in Haiti, Hawaii, Australia, and throughout Africa. **Finding your spiritual path is your unique journey in life.** A million people may adhere to the same faith, but only you can discern what holds truth and meaning for you.

Embarking on a spiritual quest is your birthright. It may not involve any established religion, or it may be firmly rooted in one religious or spiritual tradition. Perhaps it is an unfolding, changing process. At some point, your life circumstances might require you to forge a new path if a prior one becomes blocked. You may discover paths that overlap, and you may tread strange, unexpected landscapes. Ultimately, the path that leads you closer to your heart is the one that brings true happiness. **As you travel, let Spirit be your guide.**

Spiritual Exploration Questions:
- **What helps me on my spiritual journey?**
- **What moves me forward when I feel stuck?**
- **What takes me closer to my own inner knowing?**
- **What brings me true happiness and peace?**

If you're reading this book, you likely have an interest in beginning a spiritual quest or in strengthening your current spiritual practices. You wouldn't head off to another country without some thought and planning. Why not give your spiritual life the same attention … and excited anticipation. It may be the most astonishing journey you take.

Of course, like any adventure, sometimes it's the things that go wrong and the challenges we overcome that make the journey memorable. My children will always remember the trip where I locked my keys in the car at a stop off, and we had to wait for a store security guard with a slim jim to unlock the vehicle. And they laugh now about the trip where the muffler fell off the car. We brainstormed a solution along the side of the road. My youngest came up with the idea of tying the muffler back up with the cord from the sleeping bag so we could drive to the closest gas station. **Don't be discouraged if things don't go perfectly. They aren't meant to.**

A Few Suggestions in Preparation for Your Journey:

Step 1: Set Your Intention

What do you want most from your life? Are you interested in finding a spiritual teacher? Do you want to learn how to open your heart? Do you want to be of service? Do you want to learn kindness, self-love, love of others, or some other inner desire? Once you articulate your intent, reinforce it by writing it down, communicating it to others, and asking for that intent in your prayers. Many spiritual practices begin with a declaration of intention. You can then seek and ask for support in those efforts.

My intention, after a dream, was to be love and be peace at the level of my swirling atoms. It is easier to talk and write about Spirit than it is to actually live it. What does it mean to be love or be peace? If you set that sort of intention, how might it change you and your interactions with others? Setting the intention helps you to look at your life and how you are living it. If I set that intention, can I continue to argue with my ex-spouse, or will I need to find a way to do something differently? If my former spouse never changes, can I still feel loving and be peaceful?

You don't have to be a saint, monk, or spiritual guru to set a spiritual intention. Your daily challenges may be the training ground best suited for your current learning. I am a divorced woman and the mother of two children. I was fired from my job during the economic downturn. I have family members with alcohol and drug addictions. I lost a baby in a miscarriage. My biological father died in a drunk driving accident. And yet here I am, on this spiritual quest.

Declaring an intention is simply clarifying your spiritual goals. In your essence, you already exist in that space of love and peace. Spiritual tools just allow love, peace, and harmony into your awareness and daily practice. Where you put your attention and focus is what helps bring the results you desire. If you focus on wholeness, balance, and love, your day goes better. Some days are still difficult and exhausting. But the overall big picture doesn't get lost in the minutia. We learn to step back, breathe, and appreciate small tender gifts in our lives, which might be as simple as the ability to feel the morning sun on our face.

Exercise: Setting Your Intention

Take some time this week to consider what intention you'd like to set. It doesn't have to be overly complicated. Just ask your heart quietly what it needs. Then write it down. Communicate your intention to someone you'd like to support you in these efforts. It can be a supportive group, sponsor, friend, relative, spouse or partner. Include your intention in your prayers to the God, Goddess, or Spirit of your understanding. If that means a tree in your backyard, a stone you carry in your pocket, or a pole in the middle of the room, so be it.

Step 2: Make a Commitment

As most of us know, it's easy to set goals for the New Year. It's not so easy following through on those goals six months later. We may set intentions on New Year's Eve to exercise on a regular basis or eat healthy. We may even communicate these intentions to others. And then, life rolls around, we get busy, and we fall back into familiar routines and old patterns. That's why it's so important to move your spiritual intention into a concrete action plan.

What does such a commitment look like? Well, you will need daily, weekly, and monthly reminders of your goal. You will need a routine in place that reinforces the goal. You will likely need a support person or group to keep you on track and check on your progress. You also need to establish realistic, achievable goals. We all know people who show up in the gym on January 1 and go gangbusters for the first week or two. When they wear themselves out or don't see instant results, they quit. Or maybe we've tried this approach ourselves in other areas of our lives without much success.

Slow and steady wins the race. So, if you set an intention to learn to meditate or to meditate more often, you might start by locating a meditation group and making a commitment to go once a week. If a friend or partner joins you, you can then encourage each other to attend when you feel lazy or frustrated with your perceived lack of progress. Changes are often subtle, and it may take years before you realize that you've changed. Sometimes others can spot improvements in our behaviors or habitual reactions long before we even notice them.

What you don't want to do is decide that you're going to become enlightened, right now, and then start a grueling meditation schedule. It's highly improbable that such a haphazard approach will work. Most people do better with a gradual practice that they can sustain. Spiritual growth is not a race or a ribbon for your ego. Take your time, be patient, and create a routine that fits into your lifestyle. If you wanted to run a marathon, you wouldn't jog 10 miles the first day, unless you were already a seasoned runner. You might join a gym, find a trainer, and start running three times a week, gradually increasing your miles. **In Buddhism, this is referred to as finding the middle way.** Make a commitment to whatever spiritual practice you want to pursue without going to extremes on either overexertion or laziness.

When I began meditating, I started with 15 or 20 minutes of meditation before going to sleep. Later, I found a meditation group that I attended once a week. We practiced 20 minutes of sitting meditation and 20 minutes of walking meditation. That was a commitment that I was able to maintain. When I signed up for yoga, I went once a week for an hour. If you have children or busy jobs, you have to fit what you can into your schedule. Don't say it's impossible or give up. Just set small goals. Maybe every other Sunday for your spiritual practice is what you are able to do.

Be careful not to use your children or your job as an excuse. It's easy to say, "I'm too busy." But it's precisely when you are "too busy" that you are most in need of a spiritual practice. If you feel stressed, you are more apt to lose you temper, verbally snap at people, and experience higher levels of frustration and irritation. On the other hand, when you feel calm and emotionally balanced, you may listen to your children or spouse, become more playful, and feel happier; your time with others is more meaningful and generally more enjoyable.

The commitment you make may be to try a new spiritual tool for six months. The commitment may be to attend Twelve Step meetings once a week, sign up for a T'ai Chi or yoga class, or take a meditative walk each day during your lunch break or in the evening after dinner. Your commitment might be 10 minutes a day for inspirational readings. Brief reflective time might take place in your car after dropping off the kids at daycare, or on a bench during your lunch break, or while taking a bath or shower. Write your commitment on a piece of paper and tell someone who will help hold you to it. Ask for support on your journey. Pray for strength and endurance if the path gets bumpy. Make a commitment to your well-being—mental, spiritual, and physical. Remember, your commitment is to your spiritual practice and not to a specific outcome. **You may experience various positive benefits, but you can't necessarily predict where your path will lead.**

Step 3: Commit for the Long Haul

Any lasting change requires a long-term commitment. If you wanted to be physically healthier, you might have to alter eating habits, implement an exercise routine, and get rid of toxins such as cigarettes or excessive alcohol. The same is true for your spiritual life. **Walking a spiritual path is a lifetime commitment.** It's much easier when things go wrong to pick up a beer and curse at the world. But you won't get spiritually healthier with that approach. A strong dedication to continue the work of maintaining a spiritual life is necessary during rough times and when you feel like giving up. Those tough times may be the harbinger of good things to come or may bring the changes you most need.

Living a spiritual life requires a commitment for the long, arduous journey up the mountaintop. Spiritual strength isn't something anyone can hand you. Teachers point the way and offer guidance based on what they found to be useful. Discovering the path and tools that aid your spiritual growth is what your search is all about. Daily spiritual tools help in much the way eating healthy foods improves your body. But a spiritual life doesn't prevent hardships, deaths, and struggles. Everyone faces challenges—whether in the form of illness, a job loss, a divorce, or death of loved ones.

With a spiritual journey, you keep going despite obstacles. Over time, you begin to explore questions such as: What is my unique purpose or my gift? What can I contribute while I am here? How do I want to live? Is there a way to put my gifts to use for others?

Step 4: Listen to Your Heart

Answering life-affirming questions requires looking deep within your heart. Before reading further, get a piece of paper and pen. Think about your life a moment. Take 60 seconds to just breathe. Relax your body, take slow, deep breaths, and then exhale. Connect with your body. **Place a hand over your heart and breathe.** Even if your heart holds much suffering, here you are, right now. What are you doing? If you're sitting, what are you sitting on? Where are you physically: in a house, outdoors, in an airplane, hospital, or prison? Who or what is nearby? Listen to the sounds around you. Now close your eyes and feel your heart beating.

When you open your eyes, write down your dreams. If you could wave a magic wand, what would you wish for your life going forward?

Sometimes our heart hurts so deeply that nothing seems to soothe the inner ache. Being with the hurt may be all we can do truly. During those times, we can ask Spirit and friends to help carry us through the abyss. If you say, "I'm experiencing the feeling of loss," and you cradle the hurt in your heart, it allows you to just be in that space of emotional suffering without the internal stories or anything else added to it. Just acknowledge the feelings. Feelings need to be cradled much like a small, sobbing child. When hurting, often our minds want to rationalize, lash out, justify, blame, sink into self-pity, and fall prey to victim roles. We easily pick up whatever habitual mental coping mechanism we used in our past. By focusing on our heart connection, we honor our feelings. We can then stay aware of what we need in this moment.

What comes forth in the form of a heart solution isn't always easy. It may require letting go of a relationship, job, or habit that no longer serves us. Listening to our heart may feel terribly difficult at times. But ignoring what we know in our heart to be true is worse. For instance, when I hold onto a romantic relationship that isn't good for my spirit, things typically get worse and never get better until I quit grasping what wasn't right for me in the first place. There's a difference between doing the hard work that is required in any healthy relationship and a relationship or work situation that is toxic to your soul.

In one of my past dating relationships, for instance, the person drank way too much alcohol and treated women disrespectfully. He didn't share my values. I knew these things about him but chose to ignore it because I was overly impressed by his academic intelligence—high ranking in his class and in a prominent field of study. I thought I needed someone intelligent. What I learned is that academic intelligence doesn't necessarily equate to high moral or spiritual values, which are critically important to me. Academic intelligence doesn't always include traits such as kindness, honesty, and compassion. A good heart isn't measured by test grades. But it took me over a year to sort all that out. It also took the support of friends to help me find my way once I was caught up in that relationship. I spent a year ignoring the whispers of my heart. **When** the heartache gets painful enough, we can learn to wake up and pay attention.

You don't have to hate someone in order to move forward with your life. You simply need to find people who align with what you need and value in your life. It may not be easy, but it's well worth the effort to make decisions that come from a place of self-love and empowerment, rather than from a place of revenge and anger.

Ask your heart what it needs. Then stay quiet and still enough to hear the answer. Ask Spirit to guide you to the path that is for your highest good. **Only you know the answers to your heart's deepest longings.**

Take a Few Deep Breaths, Relax, and Gently Ask Your Heart the Following:

- **Where am I?**
- **Why am I here?**
- **What am I longing to do with my life?**
- **Where do I want to be?**

Step 5: Have Faith

After you set your intention, make a commitment, and listen to your heart, the next step requires what most of us fear most: surrender. We don't control the outcome. We can take positive action in the direction that calls to our heart, but we must trust the process that unfolds—which typically takes place in a time and in a way that is best for us. **Your life may head in a direction you never imagined.**

Faith is learning to trust a high power: the universe, God, Spirit, and your inner knowing. You can trust that you are loved and guided to where you need to be—even when the rational mind doesn't yet understand the why, when, where, or how. Faith, as a spiritual tool, goes beyond what you presently comprehend. Faith allows not knowing all the answers. You don't have to fully understand a situation or know how it will turn out to trust that you're doing what you need to do, today.

For example, if a person has come into your life, faith would say that there's a reason this person and you have come together. It may not be the reason you think, and it may not turn out the way you want, but there's likely something in that relationship that you need to learn or that the other person needs to learn. The same is true when a person leaves your life. The reason may not be immediately clear—and may not be understood in this lifetime. Faith admits that we don't have all the answers when something happens, but we move ahead with a willingness to continue on the journey.

Faith also allows that there are higher sources of wisdom to help us move forward in healthy ways as we learn to trust the spiritual process. Try something that calls to your heart. Meditate, attend a Wisdom Circle, practice yoga, or engage in some other spiritual practice—even if you don't have a clue what the results will be. **Stay open for guidance.**

CHAPTER 6

EVERYDAY PRACTICE:
Applying What You Learn

"It is no use walking anywhere to preach
unless our walking is our preaching."
—**Saint Francis of Assisi, (1181-1226)**

With modern living, it's easy to lose sight of the spiritual path we envision for ourselves. Even with good intentions, we may decide that we simply don't have time to apply the tools at hand. Yet, as a common Buddhist saying goes, it's when you feel that you absolutely don't have time to meditate that you most need to meditate.

Discovering the benefits of meditation, yoga, labyrinth walking, or other spiritual tools is just the beginning. Making those tools an integral part of your life is the next crucial step. Embodying what you learn and applying it to your life on an ongoing basis is necessary for your wholeness and health. Even with a crazy schedule, it's important to fit in daily spiritual practices. There were times—as a single mom working full time—when I only had five minutes before work to meditate in my car! Sometimes I fit in meditations or prayers while in the restroom or during my lunch break. But even these short respites proved helpful. Why? **Because what you do on a regular basis helps build and strengthen your inner peace.** With practice, spiritual tools that initially seem alien or extremely challenging gradually become easier. Eventually, these practices can be fully interwoven into your life.

Strengthening Your Foundation

Sometimes we think that changing our life requires a drastic, gigantic event to propel us in a new direction. Although that's true in some situations, it's certainly not always the case. Many changes occur incrementally and over long periods of time. Consider a child learning to walk. That process begins with learning to sit up, learning to rock back and forth, learning to crawl, learning to stand, and then taking the first hesitant step while holding onto something sturdy. Think about all the changes that take place over the child's next 18 years: learning to talk, read, write, drive, solve problems, and master rapidly changing technology. A spiritual life is no different. It's a continual learning process that evolves over a lifetime. **Patience and practice are helpful along the way.**

Rituals and Routines

One way to build and strengthen your spiritual foundation is to incorporate the tools into your everyday routines. Whether your tools are journaling, inspirational readings, prayer, yoga, meditation, or some other practice, make that activity part of your daily ritual. **Don't underestimate small acts. Those are the steps that can make a significant difference in your life.**

For some people, establishing spiritual routines can be challenging. Parents, for instance, are often at the mercy and whim of children whose needs are unpredictable, especially when the children are very young. Parents face many juggling acts in their day: Children get sick or injured, teenagers suddenly have a last-minute school event or transportation crisis, and youth have various school performances, sporting activities, and school-related parent meetings. Whether due to parenting, work demands, or other obligations, time constraints may absolutely be true for you. However, it's also true that you must tend to the needs of your spirit.

Spiritual practices are vital for wholeness and well-being. Your efforts may not go smoothly. But imagine the wonderful example you set for your children by taking 15 minutes to meditate before dinner preparations, or 10 minutes to journal as you drink your morning coffee, or 20 minutes for yoga stretches before going to bed. You might even get your children to join you in some of these activities. Meanwhile, you're teaching them what self-care looks like, and you're showing them that a spiritual life is a priority. By your example, they can learn how to develop healthy tools to better handle hardships in life. They may not appreciate your "time-outs," but they'll definitely benefit from your personal growth.

The same advice applies to the demands of a hectic job, caring for an elderly or sick relative, a long list of house chores, and other time-consuming life situations. Whatever your circumstances, spiritual routines help you put into practice what you've learned. Since most of us don't live in isolation, we need skills that improve our interactions with others and strengthen our ability to cope with emotional, physical, and mental difficulties. A fully embodied spiritual life is one positive way to do so.

Exercise: Bringing Your Practice to Life
Jot down one or two things you can do to bring your spiritual tools more fully into your life.

Keep the list simple and practical. If necessary, find brief increments of time and things you can do in the presence of other people.

Practice Ideas:

- Allot a few minutes each morning to read from a magazine or book that inspires you. The reading doesn't have to be long. A brief inspirational quote or paragraph can take three to five minutes for reading and reflection.
- Keep a journal near your bedside or in your car.
- Set your cell phone alarm to remind you to take three deep breaths at regular intervals throughout the day.
- Take five minutes to say a prayer each evening.
- Practice yoga or T'ai Chi daily.
- Meditate for 10 minutes after work, each morning, or right before sleep.
- Set up an email link to have daily spiritual readings delivered to your computer.
- Buy or rent a video with helpful spiritual practices and commit to watching it on a regular basis.
- Start a small group that meets once a month to practice spiritual growth through readings, meditation, labyrinth walks, or discussions of spiritual topics.

Daily Living

As noted in the *Tao Te Ching*: **"I have just three things to teach: simplicity, patience, compassion."** Spiritual tools align our heart with qualities that serve our spirit. Your meditation, retreats, or body movement tools help you discover what you need for healing and wholeness. Applying what you learn out in the world is one way to reinforce your spiritual practice. I believe that when you come to the end of your life, it will have been worthwhile because you embarked on the courageous journey of self-discovery. As Gandhi says, **"To believe in something, and not to live it, is dishonest."**

Practicing Simplicity

While sitting on my deck to write this section, a hummingbird with an iridescent green, black, and white breast buzzes near a cluster of red flowers while inserting its beak into each long red tube. Joy. Beauty. This fleeting small bird reminds me to appreciate this moment. When I reflect upon the simple pleasures in my life, they include time with my daughters, bright sunny days, walking in nature, writing, and relaxation with a cup of coffee or good book. My needs are modest. What brings me the most happiness are the people I love and time for pursuits that I truly enjoy.

At the opposite end of the spectrum, continual worry, anger, chaos, and stress take a toll on your physical and emotional health. An overly complicated lifestyle presents many obstacles to inner happiness. For instance, if we work 60 hours a week, have children and a spouse, a house to maintain, bills to pay, groceries to buy, sports activities, professional and social obligations, nightly television news, and piles of dirty laundry or dishes, we might feel hard pressed to "live a simpler life." But if we feel stressed and exhausted, then we must do something to regain our balance or we risk potential health hazards such as heart attacks, and spiritual hazards such as living an unfulfilled, empty life in pursuit of all the wrong things that don't bring us true joy.

There's an excellent book by Rick Fields, *Chop Wood, Carry Water,* which outlines the importance of blending our daily obligations with our spiritual practices. In modern Western culture, hectic work schedules or busy families don't leave a lot of time for spiritual growth. Without that spiritual advancement, however, our health, work, and families suffer. We exhaust considerable energy on merchandise purchases, raising children, romantic partnerships, and careers. How much comparable time do we take to ask what our spirit requires for real happiness? **How do we make our spiritual life part of all we do and all we are?**

Exercise: Discover Simplicity

Write down five things that bring joy to your life. If you could add something more meaningful to your life, what would it be? If you could eliminate one stressful thing, what would you get rid of? What are your highest priorities? What helps you feel more peaceful?

How Can We Practice Simplicity?

People are conditioned to focus on acquiring objects or achievements—a new job, furnishings, relationships, electronics, promotions, and so on. On a spiritual path, the lesson is to let go of what does not serve your highest good—excessive ego, greed, anger, grasping, and attachment. To apply that lesson, you may need to release those things that clutter your space, inside and out. Maybe it's the clutter in the garage or stacks of books in your living room. Maybe it's the knick-knacks on every shelf. We don't need to shop at the mall for more things. Maybe what we already have is enough. When you start to strip away externals, you begin to see more clearly what really matters.

Simplicity Questions to Explore:

- **How might I simplify my life to live it more fully and enjoy it more?**
- **How might I simplify my thoughts to better understand what matters most to me?**
- **How might I create more openness and less clutter in my living space?**
- **Is there something in my life I can do without?**
- **How might I simplify my needs and desires?**

Simplifying can be done in small, incremental doses. You might start by taking time each morning to hug your children and less time worrying about your clothing or work agenda. Look for models and examples of how to live more peacefully at work, at home, and in your community. Seek out people who share your values and have set their intention to live a simpler lifestyle. Look for small ways you can make your life less complicated and begin there.

Ideas for Introducing Simplicity Into Your Life:

- **Remove one thing from your schedule that leaves you feeling drained.**
- **Donate or discard unnecessary and excess items.**

- **Separate what you truly need from what you think you want.**
- **Take time each week to do one simple activity that brings you joy.**
- **Add a few simple pleasures back into your life.**

Practicing Patience

Spiritual tools foster patience because they employ methods that encourage you to slow down—physically, mentally, and emotionally. Yet, patience can be extremely difficult to apply in our day-to-day living. In the United States and elsewhere, we have become accustomed to prepackaged foods, microwaves, and drive-throughs for fast food, prescriptions, doughnuts, and coffee. We access vast stores of information through a click of the mouse and quick Internet searches, and we communicate via instant messaging. And often, we drive the highways at more than 70 miles per hour.

While ease and convenience can serve a useful role, there is also the downside of not pursuing something, even though it's worthwhile, because it takes time. Can you recall the last time you enjoyed a home cooked meal with real mashed potatoes, baked yams, green beans, and pie? It takes patience to peel potatoes, boil water, cook the potatoes, mix in milk and butter, and mash them. It takes time to purchase, wash, and cook fresh vegetables. And it takes patience to measure flour, mix the spices, roll out the dough, prepare the filling, and cook a pie. But anyone who enjoys good food will tell you the extra work and time is worth the effort. The same is true of your life journey. The patience and time required to explore your inner soulful promptings is worth it. You can have quick results that are less satisfying. Or you can accomplish real change and lasting benefits with patience as you travel through the process.

Life offers us many opportunities to practice patience. Parents get plenty of chances for practice with their children. Difficult bosses, co-workers, or customers test our patience at work. Spouses, lovers, relatives, and neighbors provide endless occasions to hone our patience skills. When you use spiritual tools in these circumstances, you cope better. And if you can't adequately cope, you can at least recognize that you've reached your patience limit and ask for help, rather than blowing up or acting in a way that makes the situation worse.

A spiritual practice encourages us to seek help and guidance. For instance, a relative once told me that she was driving in the car with her children, and they would not stop bickering and hollering. She finally got so frustrated that she pulled into a police station, marched the children inside, and told a police officer that her children were creating a driving safety hazard. The officer explained how dangerous it is for the driver if children are yelling and screaming. It was a funny story when she told it, but it also serves as a useful reminder. **Sometimes stopping and turning a situation over is one way to say, "I have reached my limits and I need help."** Receiving constructive guidance is preferable to continuing along on a dangerous path or letting events escalate out of control.

Using spiritual tools during stressful situations and conflicts can be extremely difficult because of our intense emotions. But it is precisely these situations where patience and practice are most needed.

Patience Tips:

- *Take a Time-Out.* **When your stress zooms beyond your current capacity to cope, take a time-out. Ask yourself what spiritual tool will help you regain your composure.**
- *Breathe.* **In the midst of conflict, you can say that you need a moment to gather your thoughts. Use that time to take a few deep breaths.**
- *Ask for Help.* **Keep a list of telephone numbers of people who have agreed to support you in a time of crisis. Your efforts to practice patience may require outside assistance.**

The goal of a spiritual practice isn't to become a saint. Sometimes the most lasting lessons come from our mistakes or the mistakes of others. We aren't meant to be perfect or to know all the answers. As poet Rainer Maria Rilke says, **"Be patient toward all that is unsolved in your heart and try to love the questions themselves."** Eventually, as we grow more patient and tolerant with ourselves, we become more accepting of the human complexity, confusion, and shortcomings of others.

Practicing Compassion

One powerful way to put your spiritual life into daily practice is to demonstrate compassion toward other people. We can show that we care about the people we interact with by maintaining compassionate thoughts, words, and actions. To quote the Dalai Lama, **"Compassion is the radicalism of our times."** Why is it radical? Because compassion changes how we treat each other, how we treat all living things on Mother Earth, and how we treat ourselves. Compassion is both personally and globally transformative. A compassionate world is a loving world.

Walking in the Shoes of Another

Compassion arises from understanding another person's predicament and putting yourself in his or her shoes. It's not the same thing as pity. Compassion goes deeper. It requires understanding something about the person or the person's life circumstances. When you listen and when you reach out, you learn. As you learn, you develop compassion. You find out more about people's losses, childhood sufferings, and fears. When you connect with people—not on a superficial level of what you want or what you can get but on the level of an open mind and open heart—you develop greater kindheartedness toward others.

No one is exempt from human sorrows. We all experience pain. People we love die. People get ill—physically, mentally, emotionally, and spiritually. People leave. People lose jobs, families, homes, and friendships. We're all in this together. Making judgments or labeling people only closes your heart to other humans. For instance, believing that all politicians and all lawyers are bad, or thinking that all Christians, all Pagans, or all Muslims are bad will prevent you from getting to know a person who has cares, worries, hopes, and dreams that may be similar to your own.

Practicing compassion can be challenging in those cases where you feel somehow mistreated. While compassion may come easily for an injured animal or a sick child, it may not come at all for someone who has harmed you or hurt someone you love. **Walking in another's shoes—knowing something about their life experiences—**

may help develop greater compassion. Recognizing your own imperfections can also give you some perspective and understanding of other people's shortcomings. Jesus talked about those without sin throwing the first stone, and he also taught forgiveness. We all have human failings. Recognizing your own faults and finding compassion for yourself, may allow greater compassion for others when they err.

One example for me arose in connection to a work-related outing. Our office planned to attend a baseball game after work. I was communicating this plan to a friend who suddenly became extremely angry. I had no idea why he was acting so verbally hurtful toward me. I live in Indiana, where the professional baseball team is named the Indians. This person was angry by the disrespect I showed Native Americans by attending this function. Because my friend was angry, he accused me of being racist. My response was to become defensive. My grandmother is Chippewa, my nephew is biracial, and my biological father's family is Vietnamese. I don't condone racism. After the conflict, I went home and meditated. I realized that because of the intensity of his anger, I had not been able to hear clearly what he was trying to communicate, which happened to be a legitimate point that got lost in the emotions. It had not occurred to me that the baseball team name was offensive. Meditation helped me work past my blinders and ask why I had not been more sensitive and aware of something that now seems obvious.

I prefer dialogue rather than anger. But I have to admit that I feel just as angry when someone uses derogatory female names or overly explicit female sexual images aimed to please men and sell movies, products, or magazines.

In the end, I had to examine my own reactions and look at the dispute from my friend's perspective. Additionally, that exchange taught me that when I'm trying to make a point with someone, my anger (even when legitimate) might make it difficult for the other person to hear what I have to say if I'm yelling or throwing around a lot of accusations. In the situation with my friend, I took time to calm my emotions. I discovered a deeper understanding of why he got angry. I allowed compassion toward my own shortcomings. After my meditation, we were able to get together and discuss what had happened. I apologized for my part. We not only resolved the conflict, but I learned a great deal in the process

Given the world's varied religious traditions and unique cultural heritages, it's easy to blunder when we meet people who have unfamiliar customs or beliefs. It takes courage to admit that you may not know enough to recognize when your views are harmful to another person or group. For instance, how much do Christians know about Muslims or Pagans? How much do heterosexual people know about homosexuals or transgender individuals? How much do Irish, Polish, or German Catholics know about Asian Buddhists?

One way to develop compassion is to seek out people who are not the same as you. Find out if you are harboring misperceptions. Compassion for yourself and compassion for others may then arise. If we were raised in another culture or environment, we might think and behave in drastically different ways than we do now.

Someone who chooses to be vegan, for instance, may not make any sense to you if your family hunts and considers animal meat a main source of protein. If you have eaten meat your entire life, you may not understand why someone else would not eat it. However, if you learn about the cruelty in animal factory farms or witness animals locked up in filthy cages, you may better understand why someone might refuse to eat meat. Or you might understand better if that person explains that he or she follows a religious or spiritual path that prohibits killing. Similarly, a vegetarian may show more compassion for a person who eats meat after learning that the person gives thanks to the animal that sacrificed its life and only eats meat from animals that ranged cage-free. Or perhaps the person's body needs something that comes from animal meat. Or maybe that person grew up on a farm, and the family's livelihood depends upon meat production.

Compassion doesn't necessarily mean you change your values; it means you have enough information to understand and allow compassion for someone else's choices. What heals us and makes us whole is mutual understanding. We all desire love, kindness, and respect. You can develop compassion and permit other people to be who they need to be. **With compassion, we gain the capacity to treat each other as worthy fellow human beings who temporarily share time together on Mother Earth.**

I don't find it easy to feel compassion for people who are intentionally cruel and practice injustice toward their fellow humans or Earth inhabitants. I'm not yet so evolved in my spiritual practice that I have reached that level of compassion. What I can try to do, though, is to feel compassion for how it must be to live as that person lives—without a loving heart and likely without much love from others. A life of fear, hatred, anger, vengeance, and violence produces great suffering in the world. That is not a life I would enjoy. **People who are filled with hate and anger are not happy**. It's also helpful to understand that people suffer from mental impairments and cultural conditioning that may result in acts of cruelty. It can't be good for their spirits to live such lives.

Many religions call for individuals to speak out against situations of injustice. Compassion doesn't mean passivity or tolerance of injustice. You can hold compassion for all who are suffering and continue to act according to your conscience. For example, you can hold compassion for a woman who is being abused. You can hold compassion for an abuser who does not know how to give or receive love in a healthy way. And you can call 911 when you witness any form of abuse. Spiritual leaders, such as Gandhi, King, and the Dalai Lama, demonstrate that **it's possible to practice compassion while also peacefully advocating for fairness and justice.**

Compassionate Communication

Compassionate communication creates healthy verbal exchanges between people. With this type of conversation, we remain mindful of what we say and how we say it. As we improve our communication skills, those around us benefit.

There are several ways to improve our communication practice. Wisdom Circles, sangha meditation groups, and Twelve Step meetings provide excellent models for learning to listen respectfully and speak only from personal experience. It's through listening that we gain greater compassion. When we pay attention to other people's stories and life experiences, we learn about their struggles. We also gain guidance on how to better handle similar situations when they occur in our life.

By speaking in "I" statements about our personal experience and feelings, we get out of the habit of blaming someone else for all our problems. Learning to speak from our heart takes courage. Being open and vulnerable with people can be scary. It's not easy to admit our fears, personal failings, hurts, and disappointments. Yet those inner reflections and honest acknowledgments are fundamental to bringing healing and wholeness into our lives.

For individuals involved in this type of exchange, the communication becomes a heart dialogue. It allows greater harmony to surface and honors the inherent dignity and value of each person. If you remain mindful of the heart message you want to communicate, and if you stay open to hearing the other person's heart message, then you begin to engage with people in new and meaningful ways. **In Buddhism, this practice is referred to as right speech, which follows from right thought; right thought follows from right understanding.** The way to right understanding is through the ability to listen to others, to correct your misperceptions and faulty mind states, and to look at other beings through the eyes of compassion.

I became aware of these methods in meditation dharma discussions. Recovery meetings are another good place to practice these skills. Now, in my current marriage, these communication skills are put to the test. Admittedly, when emotions flare and a fear or anxiety gets triggered, it's nearly impossible for me to stay calm enough to listen compassionately or to speak tenderly from my heart. I usually need a cooling-off period. Because communication in our marriage doesn't occur in a structured setting, we have to be more intentional about creating spaces or methods for talking during times of conflict. My husband and I may read our vows to reaffirm that the conflict is not bigger than our love for each other. Other times we take a walk to burn off energy and get our emotions in balance before talking. If it's still not going well, we may need separate time-outs before we try again later. We may also need counseling to help us work through our blind spots and develop better communication methods.

All the theory in the world doesn't help if you can't find ways to make your spiritual practice work in your life. As noted earlier, keep in mind that these efforts require practice and a generous allowance for "do-overs" when things fall apart. We need ongoing compassion for ourselves and for others. **No one gets it right every time.** If these skills required no effort, we wouldn't have wars and century-old conflicts. Breaking old patterns requires learning new skills and allowing ample time for implementing change. **It begins with each one of us as we learn methods to help us practice what we preach.**

Compassionate Conversation Tips:

- **Speak from your heart using "I" statements.**
- **Don't blame, ridicule, criticize, curse, or resort to sarcasm.**
- **Use courtesies such as "thank you" and "please."**
- **Show mutual respect, even during a disagreement.**
- **When things fall apart, show forgiveness of self and others.**
- **Allow for time outs and do-overs.**
- **The key to improved skills:** *practice, practice, practice.*

Acts of Kindness

Saying a kind word is easy. Being kind when we're feeling irritated or angry is much tougher. In the movie *The Razor's Edge*, based on the book by W. Somerset Maugham, the main character, Larry, reaches enlightenment in the mountains of India. When Larry returns to his guru, he is sent back down into the city. Larry is reminded by the monk, **"It is easy to be a holy man on the mountain."** Clearly, it's not so easy to be holy in our daily encounters. But by learning to nurture kindness, we bring greater happiness to ourselves and to others.

Acts of kindness allow you to experience how delightful it feels to perform generous deeds for others. When my daughters and I moved into our new home after my divorce, they rode their bicycles around exploring the neighborhood. While riding, they picked flowers and placed them in people's mailboxes to surprise them. That anonymous activity was their early Saturday morning adventure. Part of the excitement was keeping secret the identity of the flower givers, and the other part of the fun was imagining the recipients' surprise at an unexpected gift. It was a tremendous lesson for me to watch them quickly acclimate to their new environment in such a fun way.

Following my daughters' example, I decided to pick flowers from our yard to pass out to co-workers and place in a vase in the break room at work. My motive was partly selfish. I feel happier when I see flowers. My other motive was to practice giving.

I also determined to say one nice thing, each day, to a stranger in the elevator. At work, I rode 14 floors every weekday morning, afternoon for lunch, and evening when leaving. That is a lot of elevator time. I thought I would make use of that time to focus on someone other than myself. My objective was not always easy to achieve on a Monday morning when I was feeling anxious, exhausted, or discouraged. But the elevator kindness practice proved to be a worthwhile experiment. I recall one time when the favor was returned. I was feeling especially stressed, and I stood silently next to a man who suddenly looked over at me and said, **"All stress is self-imposed."** Then he nodded to himself and mumbled, "I don't know why I just said that." I smiled. This time someone else had expressed kind sentiments. I gave his statement a lot of thought over the next few months. **All I can do in any situation is**

my best. I can't control outcomes or other people. His comment reminded me that my stress reaction was actually making matters worse, not better.

It's amazingly powerful to witness the effect that kindness can have on the mindset of those around you. Kindness is a small thing. Yet, people truly appreciate such priceless gifts—sometimes more than material gifts—because kindness lifts people's burdens and brightens their moods.

I still fondly remember a small act of kindness I received many years ago on my first visit to a nearby church. My oldest daughter, then in pre-school, was feeling overwhelmed by the crowd of people. The minister had announced birthday cake for someone in the congregation, but by the time we got to the table all the cake was gone. My daughter started bawling. A woman named Susan Porter came over and asked my daughter why she was crying. Upon hearing the news that all the cake had disappeared, Susan marched into the church kitchen and quickly returned with an Oreo cookie. She said, "Here you go!" as though the lack of cake was an outrage and it was perfectly understandable why my daughter was so upset. That was an example of kindness toward a young child visiting an unfamiliar place. It made a huge impression on me as a first time visitor.

Another time, in a less pleasant situation, I saw a woman verbally berating her young boy. People were gathered for an outdoor concert. The situation was getting out of control as the woman's anger escalated and the child, who did not look to be more than 3 or 4, just stood there silently with tears rolling down his cheeks. I happened to have a balloon I had gotten for my younger daughter. I walked over and knelt down next to the child and handed him the balloon. I looked him directly in the eyes and said very calmly, "It's going to be OK." I held his gaze while the woman calmed herself. I then stood up, nodded to the woman, and walked away. I was physically shaken when I got back to my seat. It would have done no good to engage the woman in her extreme state of agitation. I did the best I could to just step between them and give the woman, and the child, a chance to breathe.

Kindness is a free gift. It doesn't have to be returned, and it doesn't require an observable effect on anyone else. I remember one time on a family vacation in New Mexico when a stranger's smile helped me. I was riding a crowded gondola up to a scenic mountain tourist spot and my oldest daughter, who was about a year old, started crying. A friendly, elderly woman, who did not speak English, started playing a game with my daughter. The woman covered her face with her hands and then suddenly opened her hands, smiling brightly, while saying what sounded like Nan Ni Ba. I don't know what language she spoke, but the gesture was the universal peek-a-boo game. I was so grateful that instead of scowling at me or at my crying child, this older woman acted in a grandmother role for a complete stranger.

Kindness Exercise

Find people this week to compliment. Try telling the store clerk that you like her dress or telling the postal carrier that you appreciate all the good news he delivers. You'll feel better for having done some small thing to benefit another person. Practice smiling at someone on the elevator or someone you pass while walking or driving.

Of course, kindness toward strangers can be easier than kind acts toward family members—especially if you experience conflict with in-laws, siblings, parents, romantic partners, or spouses. I've been guilty of such mindlessness. I recall one telephone conversation with my former spouse. I had gone outside on a work break to make the call, and we got into a fierce argument about the children's summer activities. After a few minutes of arguing, I finally hung up and said out loud, "This is crazy." At that moment, I saw a man standing nearby nodding his head in agreement. I hadn't noticed him before. It was humbling and embarrassing to be caught acting out the craziness that is so easy to spot in others. And it was craziness. I had to smile at my own willingness to engage in drama. My heated public conversation intruded on someone nearby who was just trying to enjoy his morning. I could have used that space of time outdoors more productively, perhaps meditating or breathing before making the call. I had to own my own temporary insanity and not just blame my former spouse because I fully participated in that argument.

Kindness, even in challenging circumstances, is never wasted. Regardless of whether your kind acts are rebuked, your well-being is enhanced when you know you've done the best you can with a situation. For instance, my ex-spouse and I often got into conflicts about parenting time issues. I had to continually ask myself what was truly in the best interest of the children and not get pulled into a revenge mentality based on my perception of past injustices.

Kindness didn't mean overlooking wrongs. For me, it meant letting go of the anger toward my former spouse so that I could accurately assess what my daughters needed. I had to practice kindness toward myself for all my past mistakes, kindness toward my daughters who needed time with both parents, and kindness toward my former spouse. In those circumstances, kindness meant remaining civil and taking time to listen to the truth in my heart. Sometimes kindness meant saying no with a clear conscience and without anger motivating my actions. A friend suggested that when conversations with my former spouse veered out of control, meaning that we were no longer rationally discussing but emotionally yelling, I should say, "I need to go make a bologna sandwich now." Because I don't eat bologna, it was a humorous approach. It was my friend's way of reminding me that I had the power to end the conversation until a time when my former spouse and I could communicate calmly. My friend's suggestion made me laugh. And even if I didn't say it out loud, the mental reminder proved useful.

Some people seem to know the buttons that trigger the worst in us. In the midst of strong emotions, it's best to take some time to regain your composure, seek guidance from friends or your spiritual support groups, and try to do what you know in your heart is right. Sometimes developing compassion for these individuals can help us become kinder. And sometimes, walking away from a person or situation is an act of kindness to yourself, your children, and the other person. **Be gentle and kind with yourself. All else follows from there.**

Thoughtful acts can also get us out of our self-obsessions. When we serve other people and learn about their hardships, we realize how fortunate we are to have a place to sleep, water to drink, and food to eat. There are children and adults across the world without those basic necessities. While not all of us can travel the world in service to others, there are many opportunities each day for small acts of kindness. Smiling, waving hello, and greeting people you pass, or helping someone with a door or heavy bag is service work. In a nearby restaurant, the owner has placed a sign at the front counter that states they no longer serve people who are on cell phones due to mix-ups and confusions in orders. The owner of that particular restaurant greets many customers by name and knows their favorite entries. He doesn't just serve food. He enjoys interacting with the people who enter his business. He delivers a large plate of friendliness with every order of food.

When you reach out to others, your world expands. Your thoughts are less caught up in your worries and repetitive stories. The person in line next to you at the store may have an amputated leg from military service. The person at the register may just have lost a child to cancer. You may miss someone's life story or someone's gift to you when you ignore the stranger standing by your side. **When we reach out in kindness, we connect. We care. We learn to love.**

Showing Gratitude

Expressions of gratitude can shift your entire life focus. Even at difficult times, finding one thing you are grateful for can lighten your burden. Whenever my life seems overly complicated, overwhelming, or disappointing, I try to recall something I'm grateful for. If my job, marriage, home, or community groups fall apart, I try to remember that the time I have with my daughters is a blessing. Although my daughters are now teenagers, I still give them a hug goodnight and tell them that I love them. Each time they leave to visit their dad, I work to mend any disagreements with them before they go. There's no guarantee that their presence here or my presence here will go beyond the next moment.

In the midst of hardships, expressing gratitude isn't automatic. We often need hindsight to understand how fortunate we are that we didn't get everything we wanted, when we wanted it. When we lose people close to us or experience other forms of "death" through divorce, job loss, or drastic life changes, grieving and healing may be a slow, gradual process. Most of us don't shift immediately into gratitude when we experience loss. We don't see a silver lining during what we perceive to be a horrific storm. We have to search it out or wait until enough time passes for gratitude to gently emerge.

With emotionally painful experiences, the gratitude may be for the people who help us through our grief—those people who seem to come from nowhere and offer something needed in that moment. **Sometimes the gratitude is for a feather that lands at your feet or a bird that visits as you sit outside in the yard.** During intense grief, I believe we're more open to the subtle gifts from Spirit that show up. We tap into experiences that, at other times, might never make it through our conscious awareness. **The healing we need comes—when we need it and in the way that we need it.**

When encountering hard times, repeat in your mind one thing you're grateful for. Shift your attention. Gratitude doesn't mean denying grief, pain, suffering, and loss. On the contrary, most spiritual teachers instruct that you should not close your eyes to suffering. Suffering can be a tremendous teacher. **A moment of gratitude, though, can help get you through a day that you might not otherwise get through.**

As unsettling as change can be, I believe the universe supports us during transformative experiences. After my divorce, my gratitude was for my new home. When my husband and I separated, I moved into the home of a woman whose husband had died six years prior. She needed to find new space, and I needed to begin afresh. She left a few furniture items so that she would have more room in her new place, and I was thankful to have them. She and I also took walks together after I moved in, which I am extremely grateful for. We were both grieving in our own way. I also felt grateful for my cousin, who offered many of his mother's household items when she passed away. Again, he needed to sell her house and her belongings, and I needed to supply my new home with household items at a price I could afford. In the divorce process, I discovered gratitude for all the help that came my way.

During my job search, I also received help from numerous people. Church community members formed a job search group where people could meet to discuss job goals and ways to approach the job search process. That group encouraged me to get dressed and out of the house—and helped me stay optimistic. Even with professional skills and an advanced degree, my job search process took nine months. I had been out of the work force for eight years. I now have greater empathy for others when they experience a job loss and similar or worse job-related financial struggles. I have gratitude for people who took walks with me during that time and for the people who helped with my confidence building. **The best advice I got from one friend was, "Keep an open mind."** If I went to a job interview that didn't seem to go well, she would remind me to wait and see. When I finally received a job offer for a job that I didn't want, friends told me to give it a try. We can't always accurately assess what is best for us when fear and worry take hold. When I finally began working, I felt frazzled and exhausted. But I tried to remember gratitude for income, for the new friends I was meeting, and for the new learning experiences.

Gratitude is an ongoing process of giving thanks even when things are not going exactly as we like. A job may mean stress, and a lack of a job may mean even more stress. A relationship may bring heartache, and a lack of a relationship may bring loneliness. New challenges arrive daily. Gratitude for being alive may be your only constant. Thankfulness for pleasant weather when it arrives or gratitude for drinking water (assuming you have clean water to drink) is a good practice. Gaining clarity about our needs, rather than our wants, also assists with gratitude. Staying open to what we can't yet envision for our lives also brings greater gratitude. There are people and places experiencing wars, bombs dropping on their homes, preventable diseases, overpopulation and limited resources, and violent crimes that go unpunished.

At work one time, a client on the telephone told me that I was very kind. He was passing heartfelt compliments my way in an upbeat, cheerful way. Later in the conversation, I learned that he had been in a car accident that crushed his ankles. He not only survived that wreck, but he turned his attention in this conversation toward complimenting me. It takes inner strength to turn your focus from your own concerns long enough to observe other people and to thank them for their many gifts.

Ways to Practice Gratitude:

- **Write your troubles on a piece of paper and ask the universe to hold them for you long enough for you to find and appreciate one gift in your life.**
- **Make a gratitude list before you go to sleep or each morning when you wake.**
- **Keep a gratitude journal.**
- **Write notes to friends to express your appreciation for their presence in your life.**
- **Hug your children, spouse, lover, or friends.**

Additional Ways to Practice Gratitude:

- Sit in the sun, take a deep breath, take a sip of water, and say thank you.
- Stand under a tree and say thank you.
- Look up at the sky and say thank you.
- Send a prayer of thanks for another day.

CHAPTER 7

BUILDING COMMUNITY:
Expanding the Circle

"The twentieth century was the century
of individualism, but we don't want that anymore.
Now we try to live as a community."
—Thich Nhat Hanh, Buddhist monk

Sometimes we forget that we're all in this spinning, loving, and chaotic world together. We also depend on each other more than we acknowledge. Someone plants and grows the food you consume, builds your house or apartment, assembles your appliances and computer gadgets, repairs your car, bus, or bicycle, paves the streets, and connects the pipes so you have water to drink—if you're fortunate enough to live where there is water piped into homes.

We may think that because we pay for some services, we're powerful or independent. But do we take time to say thank you for all that we receive? Do we realize that cash is but a small part of the exchange? We rely on doctors, nurses, electricians, farmers, carpenters, schoolteachers, attorneys, mechanics, computer technicians, plumbers, and so on. Individually, we are lost. **I believe one of our greatest lessons is to truly understand that we must help one another.**

In community, we care for each other—providing necessary strength and support during life challenges. The group cradles us in times of sorrow and lifts us up in times of celebration. Joining a community introduces you to people with greater experience who can guide you. Such a group can also provide models for alternative ways of living and keep you committed to your own spiritual practice. **Through community participation, our individual roles gradually become more deeply connected to the bigger picture.**

Not long ago, I had a dream in which I was given a test. When I sat down, I saw that the test paper had been torn in half. I asked but could find no one who had the other half. I was handed a pencil and went back to my seat. When I woke up, I was worried about how I could possibly offer "correct" answers on spiritual matters if I didn't even know the questions. For me, much of this dream was about letting go of "knowing." Another part was linked to my inner journey and the need to fill in the blanks for my own questions and answers, rather than letting other people do that for me. Deep soul searching work is essentially a solitary endeavor.

Paradoxically, the final insight from the dream was how community helps contribute to our growing understanding of both the questions we ask and the answers we seek. No one person has all the answers. When we're immersed in conflict or extreme hardships, for instance, our friends, family members, and spiritual support groups can show us how to navigate through our confusion. It's simply not possible to always remain objective when we're emotionally entangled in a situation. Other people may identify what needs to change—whether in our thinking or behavior. Likewise, with pressing global questions, many people working together can fill in the blanks to solve problems and find positive answers. **We need to stay open to both the questions and answers that arise.**

Support for the Journey

When my friend Tom suffered a stroke (I mentioned his story in Chapter 3), his wife Stephanie asked for prayers, healing energy, and songs from their varied community groups. They received physical, emotional, and spiritual care from family members and from friends in their art, theatre, church, neighborhood, and chorus communities. People organized meals, hospital visitations, cat feedings, healing sessions, music therapy, house cleaning, and other forms of ongoing support. It was amazing to watch individuals from diverse groups coming together during the crisis to help in myriad ways.

That experience reminded me that a spiritual community is not limited only to members of a specific organized religion. Various groups can serve a spiritual role in people's lives. In this case, the friends who are artists and singers expressed their spirituality through their creative expressions. Other friends brought healing herbs, songs, and stones. Some family members prayed on a rosary while friends chanted, meditated, or drummed as a form of prayer. Friends who are Jewish, Christian, Native American, Unitarian Universalist, Pagan, Goddess, Wiccan, nondenominational, and shamans also offered prayers. The commonality was love for Tom and Stephanie in their time of enormous suffering and great need.

Another meaningful community event I witnessed involved ceremonies in the American Indian tradition. I was invited to join a Vision Quest with individuals who had spent a year or more planning, praying, and preparing for this significant ceremony. I arrived in Colorado with the intent to support a friend going on the hill for her Vision Quest. I was told that during my friend's Vision Quest, she would spend days in a secluded location in the hills praying to Spirit and listening for Spirit's guidance. Individuals who go on Vision Quests are never truly alone because the community supports them through prayers, rituals, and welcoming ceremonies upon return.

While observing the ceremonies for my friend's Vision Quest, I mentioned to some elder women the solo faith quest I had taken in Southern Indiana (discussed in the solo retreats section of Chapter 4). I mentioned the horrible storm and how awful that experience had been. After listening to my story, these women invited me to go on a Vision Quest. I didn't have the things many participants normally take with them: prayer flags, a Sacred Pipe, and songs passed on from the ancestors. I was reluctant to go and gave a long list of reasons why I couldn't do it: I had come to support someone while she went on her Vision Quest; I didn't have the right clothes; I wasn't prepared; I didn't have any of the traditional items needed for a Vision Quest. The women who were counseling me said that I could support another person while on my own Vision Quest and that they could get me the necessary items. Still I resisted.

Nevertheless, these women knew that my real reason for not wanting to go on a Vision Quest was that I felt absolutely terrified. They also recognized that I needed to face those fears and go on a Vision Quest—only this time with community support. The women gathered for me a string of tobacco prayer bundles, a ceremonial dress, and a Sacred Pipe.

For a Vision Quest, small tobacco bundles are made all year with prayers attached to each one. A woman in the group had decided not to go on the hill this year. She offered me her prayer bundles, along with all the work, effort, and prayers she had put into them. Another woman found me a ceremonial dress. A third woman, whom I admire and consult with to this day, offered me the use of her Sacred Pipe. It is humbling to receive gifts of such spiritual import. Someone allowing you to take his or her Sacred

Pipe on a Vision Quest is equivalent to the pope giving you his personal rosary or cross that he has carried, held, and prayed over and letting you to take it on a religious pilgrimage and then return it afterward. I'm not sure even that comparison does justice to the importance of the Sacred Pipe in the American Indian traditions. The Sacred Pipe is a direct link to Spirit. Such gifts are not given lightly.

The entire community then walked me, and the others going on Vision Quests, to various locations on the hill. The community kept a fire burning throughout the night and held us in prayers and songs. With this Vision Quest, the community gave me the nonmaterial gifts of faith, trust, support, and safety. I prayed to the directions. I sang. I gave thanks for all the gifts that were offered so freely when I had none of the things I needed. The Vision Quest, even during a light rainstorm, felt peaceful and gentle.

The lesson I received is that when we care for each other—and allow others to care for us—we assist each other along the journey. **As Spirit guides us, we recognize that we're part of the greater whole.** I'm more aware now of the connected threads woven through each of our lives. We come to Earth helpless, as babies. We couldn't survive without the gifts of sun, rain, air, earth, nourishment, and shelter. The temple we walk each day is Mother Earth. Prayer is our song, along with the words we speak. What we say and what we do affects all other threads of existence. Duty means taking your part in community and contributing to the common good.

When we acknowledge these gifts and say thank you for all we receive, we become more than our small, individual selves. We learn how to live collectively. We understand how our role contributes to the greater whole, and we walk our path with gratitude.

Shared Values

When seeking a spiritual community, thoughtfully assess your values, intentions, and needs. Then look for a group that demonstrates those traits and fulfills those desires. Groups establish their values in a variety of ways. They may adopt a shared set of principles, a mission statement, a covenant, a set of commandments or precepts, or a list of steps and beliefs. Religious or spiritual texts are often used for guidance. Additionally, values might be expressed through commonly recognized phrases, readings, songs, rituals, and ceremonies.

In any group, healthy communication, respect, honesty, and financial transparency are key ingredients to a properly functioning system. Leadership roles based on the needs and input of the community help prevent abuse of power and ego struggles. It's also important that groups adopt constructive methods for resolving conflicts, which inevitably arise when people get together.

Before joining, learn as much as you can about the community. For instance, certain religious and spiritual groups readily accept individuals who are exploring several spiritual paths. Other groups may be working to preserve and protect their specific traditions. Some groups are open, and others have membership restrictions.

I recall one experience with a restricted-membership group. A close family member of mine was missing. At the time, this family member was under the influence of an alcohol and crack cocaine addiction. In desperation, I searched out and found a Narcotics Anonymous (NA) meeting. The people were all very friendly and respectful toward me. But after the meeting, someone explained that the group I needed was Al-Anon, which is intended for family members of those with an alcohol addiction. The NA meeting was intended to be exclusively for people with narcotic addictions so they could have a safe, anonymous space to address their addiction issues.

The restrictions served the group's purpose. I had unknowingly attended the wrong group for my needs.

It's vital for a new community to feel welcoming. A group that's too rigid or too exclusive may not give a newcomer the necessary support. Sometimes it helps to visit a few different groups to find the one that feels right.

The first couple of Al-Anon meetings I attended didn't feel comfortable for me. They were large groups that felt overwhelming. A meeting I tried later was a smaller group that consisted of mostly older women who maintained their sense of humor and lightheartedness. These women didn't mince words; they spoke their truth from many years of hard-earned wisdom. For my needs at the time, that group was a good fit.

Joining a group that welcomes your contributions and shares your vision can be invaluable. Such a group reminds you that you're not alone. **When times get tough, a community that shares a common, larger purpose can keep your spirit afloat.**

Community Questions to Ask:

- **What's important to me in a spiritual community?**
- **Do I desire wisdom teachings, social companionship, encouragement, or additional training in some area?**
- **Do I want personal challenges and growth?**
- **Do I need solace and healing?**
- **Do I prefer large social groups or small, intimate groups?**
- **Do I like clear guidelines, structure, and well-articulated expectations or loose, free-flowing activities?**

Our Common Humanity

Most groups occasionally face personality conflicts, mistakes, and ego/power struggles. Don't expect a group—even a religious or spiritual community—to be without flaws. Groups are made up of human beings who have strengths and weaknesses. Working together to build consensus, following respectful listening and speaking practices, and having a willingness to accept change are hallmarks of a strong and lasting community.

Find a group that recognizes these difficulties rather than denying their existence. Healthy groups are more likely to have tools in place to prevent the escalation of interpersonal problems. Such practices may include speaking from the heart and only from personal experience rather than criticizing or blaming someone else. Seek groups that have a process for addressing issues as they arise and for ensuring that all voices are heard.

These methods might include a democratic voting mechanism for decisions, clear guidelines or covenants for acceptable behavior, and a procedure such as mediation with a trained facilitator for dealing with conflicts in a thoughtful and fair manner. **Healthy problem solving incorporates mutual respect and deep listening.** If no conflict resolution process is in place, discuss what might be useful within the group structure for resolving disputes. There are many healthy models to choose from. Make sure the group you select shows compassion for human shortcomings within the larger framework of the group purpose.

Sometimes people become disillusioned when they learn that spiritual and religious groups have the same issues and problems faced by everyone else they know: jealousy, fear, anger, impatience, and power struggles. A large group with diverse views may encounter even more challenges as each person brings his or her issues and roles from childhood into the group setting. If the group is adhering to principles that guide individuals toward wholeness, it can help foster healthy interactions. **A community committed to developing respectful communication skills can lead toward creating a supportive environment.** The common goals, purpose, and mission must be stronger than individual failings and personalities. A healthy community teaches us how to live with each other, how to solve problems without violence, and how to grow into the caring people we know ourselves to be. Everyone in the community then benefits from working together to find positive solutions to challenges that arise. Any group that believes itself superior to other groups falls into the realm of ego rather than Spirit.

Groups that historically faced persecution—or continue to face discrimination and hatred—may not as readily welcome outsiders. Respect the boundaries a group has in place, even if you don't immediately understand the reasons. The gates may open more freely when marginalized groups receive the same respect and recognition as the dominant religions. Until then, go where you are called but don't force yourself into any group.

An Open Mind

We probably believe we're open-minded—until we get into a disagreement with someone. Keeping an open mind toward new ideas and divergent beliefs can be frightening. Yet, an open mind is essential when exploring faith communities. What initially sounds strange or weird may actually lead to your spiritual growth.

Many years ago, I was writing an article on someone who had transitioned from male to female. As part of the research for the story, the person asked me to attend a party where I could meet other transgender individuals. All I had in my knowledge base at that time came from drag queen images in movies. As a married woman with two young children, I felt out of my comfort zone. Despite my strong fears of the unknown, I agreed to go to the party.

What I found there surprised me. The people were no different from any other group of middle-aged individuals getting together for a social gathering. Some had brought their children with them, some were introverts and appeared more interested in reading a news magazine or discussing recent technology advances than in casual party banter, some were sociable and chatty as they nibbled on pretzels or cheese and crackers, some drank ice water or tea, and some had a bottle of beer or glass of wine. All in all, it was a non-eventful gathering. Over time, I learned much more about the person I was interviewing, and we became friends. That friendship would not have happened had I been unwilling to visit a setting outside my comfort zone. The unfamiliar is what taught me about my own misperceptions. I'm embarrassed now to share those earlier misperceptions. **But how will we grow spiritually if we don't admit our shortcomings and learn from them?**

I've experienced a similar fearful reaction with my introduction to unfamiliar spiritual practices and religious groups. The first time I went to a Goddess Circle, I didn't know what to expect; I also didn't know the people well. Initially, I felt incredibly nervous. But after attending that group a number of times, I started to feel more comfortable. I also began to learn about the feminine aspects of the divine. Today, some of my closest friends are a group of women who believe in the Feminine Divine and Goddess spirituality. These women are artists, mothers, teachers, musicians, and so on. They simply choose to honor a female, life giving, nurturing form of Spirit—rather than a vengeful, male god that incites or justifies wars.

When I was invited to a shamanism workshop, I again felt slightly panicked. (I discussed some of these experiences in Chapter 4). Growing up in a working-class neighborhood outside of Detroit, many spiritual concepts simply never existed in my vocabulary or personal experience. What I learned after attending shamanism sessions is that a shaman is a healer who typically uses drums, rattles, herbs, chants, and contact with the Spirit realm in the healing process. At one of the workshops, I noticed a couple with their son: He appeared to be mildly autistic and in his early 20s. The family looked joyous; they had found something they could do together that the son truly enjoyed. It was wonderful to watch them. As I also mentioned earlier of my own experience, I gained enormous healing from my willingness to explore this practice. I now incorporate the drumming and meditative aspects into my own spiritual rituals.

An unfamiliar religious or spiritual community may capture your heart once you try it. **Don't let fear of the unknown prevent your explorations.** The mind may skeptically ask: What is a sangha? What is Reiki? What we don't understand we tend to fear, judge, and dismiss. By keeping an open mind, we remain curious. Gradually, we learn to approach the mysterious unknown with a greater sense of wonder rather than dread.

A spiritual or religious community should also maintain an open mind. A group shouldn't get into the habit of placing its beliefs above the practices and beliefs of other groups. What feels like a "right" path for some people is not the only or best path for everyone else on this planet. To stay relevant, a group may also need to evolve as times change.

During my visits to Colorado, the Native American ceremonies involved cutting down a tree that was then brought to the community. The tree may have served as a connection between people, nature, and Spirit. In the past, the community may have used trees as firewood for cooking the food and as a source of heat to keep people alive during the winter. One time while I was there, the children questioned this practice of cutting down a tree as part of the sacred ceremonies. "There are so few trees, why is the community cutting one down for the ceremony? Shouldn't we be planting trees?" they asked. To his credit, the spiritual leader of that community took the children's questions seriously. The group decided to plant a tree as part of their ceremony that summer and not cut one down. Such a decision can send ripples of terror through a community that has been accustomed to doing things a certain way. Most groups do not easily welcome change.

It takes courage to examine the reasons for an action and to thoughtfully assess: Is the action helpful or harmful, and what effect will the action have seven generations out? My definition of sin would be to promote an action that is known to cause harm. For instance, if people are at risk of AIDS and unwanted pregnancies for the lack of birth control, I think it is unconscionable to use religion in a way that harms these individuals. The same is true for religions that promote hate or violence toward any person or group. If love is the basis of a spiritual life, then religious and spiritual groups must learn to lover better. Groups must keep an open mind on the changing landscape that represents this time and this place—rather than blindly following practices that no longer address current needs. **Love must be the guiding force that directs individual and group actions.**

We have not yet begun to explore the Spirit realm of all life forms on this planet—the spirit of trees, the living essence of Earth herself, and the self-healing energy within our own human matrix. We are continually learning from each other and the world around us. We teach each other as we go. As you venture into new spiritual communities or work within your present community, let your heart and Spirit lead you. **A healthy family, loving neighborhood, and peaceful world community is our destination.**

Mentors, Sponsors, and Teachers

In most jobs, a person in training is placed with a more experienced, knowledgeable, or advanced person in that field. The same principle holds true for a spiritual journey. Someone further along on that path can provide guidance, support, and wisdom for a person who is just starting out.

People who serve as mentors, sponsors, and teachers may be leaders in a spiritual or religious community, or they may be people with extensive experience in an area that's of interest to you. I tend to seek advice from individuals who are a decade older because they've been through my life stage already and can reflect back on how they managed. Someone who is a grandparent, for instance, can offer guidance to a new mom with a sick baby. In the same way, someone who has practiced meditation for many years or who has a well-established prayer practice may be able to offer useful suggestions to someone who is new at it and feeling lost or confused.

When seeking a mentor, sponsor, or teacher, find someone whose life you admire. Admiration shouldn't be based on his or her material acquisitions or popularity. Seek someone who embodies the deeper values you wish to emulate. This person doesn't have to be perfect;

everyone has human shortcomings. Simply be intentional about finding a mentor, sponsor, or teacher who has more experience or wisdom in an area you wish to grow in.

Mentor, Sponsor, Teacher Considerations:

- **Does the person exhibit inner strength, calm thinking, and a commitment to his or her own personal growth?**
- **Does the person have an established spiritual practice?**
- **Do you need someone to listen to you, console you, nudge you, motivate you, or encourage you to change?**

Don't expect to get everything you desire from one person. Mentors, sponsors, and teachers demonstrate ways to handle life's challenges. But sometimes they teach us by showing us what not to do in a given situation. They also model their humanity when they let others know of their mistakes and their lessons from those errors. For example, in recovery programs, sponsors might share personal stories about how their lives became unmanageable, situations where they had to make amends, and how they put the recovery steps into daily practice. **Such honest sharing reminds us that those we admire are human.**

As the eldest child in an alcoholic home, I often thought I had to be perfect. In high school, I took great pains with my hair and my clothes. While we may be perfect in the eyes of Spirit, on a human level we all make mistakes. We can gain enormous relief in knowing that human perfection is never asked of us. Mistakes bring greater compassion and empathy for others who make similar errors.

We also learn by discovering what doesn't work well in our lives. We can then shift our attention to what does add to our happiness. Meanwhile, we do the best we can each day. Sometimes we end up teaching just by the questions we ask. The student learns from the teacher, the teacher learns from the student, and we all grow in the process. **Forgiveness—of self and others—is part and parcel of the human experience.**

Friendships

Aligning ourselves with friends who support our highest aspirations will greatly benefit us when we falter. Friends see our blind spots and patterns in a way that we may miss. Reaching out for help is critical when we find ourselves getting off track. In recovery groups, members talk about the need to pick up the telephone and make a call during a crisis, and if the first person doesn't answer, go down the list until someone does. Our friends encourage us to persevere. They tell us not to give up. In some cases, they help us see the humor in our predicaments. When you reach out to a friend and ask for guidance, you help your friend grow in his or her thinking and you let your friend share his or her present level of understanding.

Friends also let us know that we're not alone. They lend a shoulder to cry on as well as reminding us of our commitments. They may recognize when we're fooling ourselves or when we're caught up in old childhood storylines—that internal dialogue that says we're not worthy or not loved or not good enough. Friends let us know that we're loved, even when we're not feeling calm or lovable. **Just hearing a friend say, "Hang in there," can get us through a tough day.**

In the play *Twelve Angry Men*, it took a protracted conversation between 12 jurors in a homicide trial to bring out each other's strengths, weaknesses, flawed reasoning, and prejudices. With only our own opinion, we may overlook a vital piece of information or miss another vantage point of the big picture. A variety of perspectives and insights must be brought to the collective table. We may need a friend who is analytical, a friend who is a good listener, and a friend who doesn't let us get away with self-deception. When we associate with a mix of people unlike ourselves, we expand our learning.

By cultivating friendships across a broad range of religious and spiritual belief systems, we not only gain knowledge about those divergent practices, we also recognize that our love for humanity extends beyond any labels. When a person is your friend, you care for that person's happiness. When that person gets sick or suffers a loss, you want to help. Our friendships bond us in a way that is stronger and sturdier than any dogma. We don't have to build walls and manufacture weapons to keep people out. We have to build bridges of understanding, compassion, and true friendship—regardless of race, religion, creed, gender, age, nationality, or geographic place of birth.

Friends hold a special place in our hearts. We need more friends. That may mean reaching out to others, even when we're afraid. As A.A. Milne says in Winnie-the-Pooh, **"You can't stay in your corner of the Forest waiting for others to come to you. You have to go to them sometimes."**

CONCLUSION

THE PATH FORWARD:
Living a New Vision

"Be the change you want to see in the world."
—Attributed to Mahatma Gandhi

Why is it so necessary to find spiritual tools and apply them to your life? One imperative reason is that this planet and the people on it need healing. Look at what we've done without spiritual practices and without deep, soul-searching healing. Look at the children in Haiti, in Cambodia, in India, in poverty-stricken areas in the United States and in Afghanistan. Do you love these young individuals? Are all people truly connected as our brothers and sisters on Mother Earth? Are we conscious of the effect of our actions on children living in war-torn cities, children in hospitals because of environmental pollutants that are toxic to their young bodies, and children with parents who rage against each other verbally and physically? Use of spiritual tools is like having a compass or GPS to point the way when we're lost and to keep us headed in a healthy direction.

When you acquire tools that place your heart and mind in alignment with Spirit, you gain inner strength. That means you have the strength to say "No" to those behaviors that don't bring wholeness and the strength to say "Yes" to those behaviors that remind you of your enormous capacity for love—even when all else around you flies apart in a violent whirl. On a spiritual path, you walk with purpose and seek that which serves your soul. You care about healing the heart of others and you change directions when the current path is violent or destructive. If your life is motivated by greed, ego, hatred, fear, revenge, or anger, it's time to find another path. On a spiritual journey, you travel with compassion, joy, and gratitude. You appreciate the beauty and preciousness of life.

Never doubt the impact of your inner spiritual work—even if you don't always see tangible results. By living with wholeness of mind, body, and spirit, you enjoy a healthier and happier life. You live in a way that has meaning and purpose. Perhaps you're called to teach, to model alternatives to the status quo, to encourage and inspire others, or to seek out constructive solutions to vexing problems. Whatever worldly path you travel, spiritual tools guide the inner promptings of your soul. **Following a life of Spirit is a worthy pursuit.**

Healing

We're here on Earth so briefly; yet, we have the capacity to create so much that is beautiful, tender, and good.

Sit near a tree and appreciate its cool shade on a sweltering summer day; embrace calm moments while watching squirrels frolic and race about nearby. Learn from the tree: Deep roots ground you, a sturdy trunk offers strength, branches reach toward the sky, leaves shimmer in the sunlight, and colorful leaves eventually fall away to become something new. When you align your spirit with that tree, you understand all there is to know. Problems are not so complicated; we've created many of the world's problems ourselves. Simple lives result in less complicated solutions: Share resources with those in need; show compassion; practice gratitude for daily gifts; live this moment; stay in today; and release expectations, agendas, power struggles, excessive ego, fear, and greed. Love your neighbor (and the stranger) as yourself. Do no harm.

Surrender and allow faith to kick in. **Remind yourself: I can't do everything, but I can offer my one gift.** If you don't know what to do or how to do it, ask for guidance. "Ask and it shall be given to you." (Matthew 7:7.) Let go of the how and when and pray instead for an open heart. You'll receive the teachers you need, the situations you need, and the healing you require. Ask to be of service. The opportunity will arrive. By committing to a spiritual life, you acknowledge what's at stake—your happiness, the happiness of future generations, and the happiness of all living entities. **Your thoughts, intentions, and prayers affect all that you are and all that you do.**

When we care about the world, we use tools that help our thoughts stay loving, our words stay true, and our spirits stay strong. We use tools that return our minds to loving-kindness during struggles. We use tools that help us parent our children and love our spouses, partners, relatives, co-workers, and neighbors. We then begin to model healthy behavior and make wiser decisions. As we improve the quality of our lives, we teach each other through our personal practice. We learn how to stay connected to our hearts.

Every day offers occasions to observe areas of growth and discard old patterns that no longer serve your deeper intentions. Your practice will bring more questions. Your practice will bring answers from your heart, body, mind, and spirit. When you're no longer governed from the outside, you're free. **In the end, no book or practice will matter as much as the moments you fully lived and loved while here on this planet.**

Healing Questions to Ponder:

- **What are my life priorities?**
- **When faced with tragedy, what's important to me?**
- **What needs healing?**
- **How do I want to be in the world—regardless of what anyone else does?**

Making a Change

We're all responsible for the love we demonstrate in our lives. Blaming others won't move you forward in a positive way. Individually and collectively, we're asked to grow and evolve. Bring inner peace into your life and build bridges of peace with others. **Don't wait for some other person or religious leader to show you the way.**

Each person must now take an active leadership role in his or her own life. Each of us must share a more hopeful message in word and deed. Each person must contribute to the global effort of healing our world community. We are the change. We must share what we learn with others. As we raise our standards, we bring forth personal and global evolution. Each day we ask for our lives to become whole, free, loving, and strong—not for our own sake alone, but for the sake of the entire planet. When aligned with Spirit, you greatly benefit the larger whole.

The world desperately needs people who understand how to stay centered and peaceful during conflicts. We need people who have learned to heal their deepest wounds. Positive changes are made by daily choices, words that are spoken, products that are purchased, and ways that love is expressed. Infinite possibilities exist for your life as you allow endless supplies of love to be a source of healing, growth, and happiness for yourself and for others. With practice, you can reach out more readily to those who are suffering. You'll laugh more easily, live more fully, and realize you're alive, today. **Your prayers for guidance are heard and answered.**

Thoughts to Help with Change:

- **Pay attention.**
- **Don't worry so much.**
- **Let go.**
- **Be.**
- **Live.**
- **Love.**
- **Keep moving forward.**
- **Grow.**
- **Be prepared today to die, knowing you have done your best.**
- **Know you are loved.**
- **Know you are whole.**

That is how we travel a spiritual journey together, with enormous gratitude for the privilege of being alive to both the celebrations and sorrows of life. **Your life and how you live it is your greatest spiritual practice.**

Spiritual Activism

Giving back is a wonderful way to demonstrate gratitude for all you've received. You can put your spiritual values into practice through community outreach efforts. When Vietnamese monk Thich Nhat Hanh reached out to assist all sides during the Vietnam War, the term *Engaged Buddhism* was coined. With any spiritual practice, there is a need to face suffering and to help create a better future for our children. Community service work doesn't mean having pity for or doing for another person. Service for others entails asking what someone needs, listening to their concerns, and reaching out from a place of wisdom to the root causes of problems. With that intention, you share your passion and talents in a way that empowers others to recognize their own gifts.

Whatever your unique ability, you can give that skill in service to others. Civic engagement doesn't have to be overly complicated. It doesn't demand travel to another country and extensive monetary contributions, although both of those methods can be helpful. Outreach may be offering to drive someone to a group event or sharing spiritual workshop information with a friend. Making coffee or tea for a group, grocery shopping for a neighbor, or walking in the park with someone who is grieving can be useful service work. Volunteering with youth in your community or taking time to listen to individuals who are less fortunate is beneficial work. Maybe listening is the gift you offer. Maybe teaching someone to read is your gift. Maybe music is your offering. Maybe sharing lessons that you've learned from suffering is your gift. My writing is the gift I share. At the end of this book, you'll find information on an organization that is reforesting Haiti. A percentage of the profits from this book go to support the efforts of that organization.

Use your gifts to brighten the world. If you're technology savvy, for instance, you have a whole host of ways to serve others. When exploring spiritual activism, think outside the box. There are motorcycle riding groups that raise money for children's hospitals, yoga groups that give time and money for nonprofit causes in poor countries, meditation groups that donate computers to schoolchildren in Haiti, and neighborhood groups that develop community gardens and eliminate invasive plant species from nearby parks. Creative solutions present themselves when you tap into the wellspring of your talents.

Spiritual Activism Questions to Ask Yourself:

- **What can I contribute to my community?**
- **What is my strength, interest, or skill set?**
- **Am I reaching out to children and youth or the elderly?**
- **Am I connecting with my local community organizations?**
- **Which issues spark my deepest passion?**

Groups are strengthened by individual member contributions. You'll discover that as you give freely of your time and talents, you reap unexpected benefits such as friendships, increased skills, self-growth, confidence, and sense of purpose. Giving is hugely beneficial when it comes from a place of love and enthusiasm, rather than from a sense of obligation or guilt. Imagine the miraculous community improvements we can implement as we learn to care deeply for one another. Look what happens when we hug someone who is feeling lost, hold someone's hand who is grieving, bring flowers from our garden for someone who is ill, or listen to someone talk about his or her day.

All people experience fears, losses, and stress. How might you help a friend, neighbor, or family member who is struggling? Sometimes, just letting people know that you care about them and that they're loved can heal hearts, bodies, spirits, and mind. There's no greater healing than through love. As noted by Starhawk, "All began in love, all seeks to return in love. Love is the law, the teacher of wisdom, and the great revealer of mysteries."

Spiritual and religious practices teach us that each person caring for one another is the path. On a spiritual journey, we travel a course that increases our capacity to demonstrate small acts of generosity and love.

When my children were young, I watched them playing a game at the nearby neighborhood park with some other children. They were taking turns jumping down from the jungle gym. One child climbed back up whenever another child had jumped down. I asked my daughter what they were playing. She said, "People come down from the stars, and when one jumps down to help those on Earth, the other one goes up to help from the stars." I remember thinking, who knows? Maybe death is just someone helping from a different location or in a different mode. **Maybe we're all just helping each other along the journey.**

May it be so.

RELATED READING

Andrews, Ted. *Animal Speak: The Spiritual & Magical Powers of Creatures Great & Small.* St. Paul, Minn.: Llewellyn Publications, 2004.

Avila, Elena, and Joy Parker. *Woman Who Glows in the Dark: A Curandera Reveals Traditional* Aztec Secrets of Physical and Spiritual Health. New York: J.P. Tarcher/Putnam, 2000.

Awiakta, Marilou. *Selu: Seeking the Corn-Mother's Wisdom.* Golden, Colo.: Fulcrum Publishing, 1994.

Bear Heart, and Molly Larkin. *The Wind Is My Mother: The Life and Teachings of a Native American Shaman.* New York: Clarkson Potter, 1996.

Bradford, Michael. *The Healing Energy of Your Hands.* Freedom, Calif.: The Crossing Press, 1995.

Budapest, Zsuzsanna Emese. *The Holy Book of Women's Mysteries.* Berkeley, Calif.: Wingbow Press, 1989.

Cameron, Julia. *The Artist's Way: A Spiritual Path to Higher Creativity.* New York: J.P. Tarcher/Putnam, 2002.

Cameron, Julia. *The Complete Artist's Way: Creativity as a Spiritual Practice.* New York: Jeremy P. Tarcher/Penguin, 2007.

Chödrön, Pema. *The Places That Scare You: A Guide to Fearlessness in Difficult Times.* Boston: Shambhala Publications, 2007.

Chopra, Deepak. *The Way of the Wizard: Twenty Spiritual Lessons in Creating the Life You Want.* New York: Harmony Books, 1995.

Courage to Change: One Day at a Time in Al-Anon II. New York: Al-Anon Family Group Headquarters, 1992.

Curry, Helen. *The Way of the Labyrinth: A Powerful Meditation for Everyday Life.* New York: Penguin Compass, 2000.

Dalai Lama, *How to Practice: The Way to a Meaningful Life*. Waterville, Maine: Thorndike Press, 2002.

Dyer, Wayne W. *The Power of Intention: Learning to Co-create Your World Your Way*. Hay House, Inc., 2004.

Fields, Rick. *Chop Wood, Carry Water: A Guide to Finding Spiritual Fulfillment in Everyday Life*. Los Angeles: Jeremy P. Tarcher/Putnam, 1984.

Garfield, Charles A., Cindy Spring, and Sedonia Cahill. *Wisdom Circles: A Guide to Self-Discovery and Community Building in Small Groups*. New York: Hyperion Books, 1998.

Gawain, Shakti. *Meditations: Creative Visualization and Meditation Exercises to Enrich Your Life*. Novato, Calif.: New World Library, 2002.

Hanh, Thich Nhát. *Peace Is Every Step: The Path of Mindfulness in Everyday Life*. New York: Bantam, 1992.

Harner, Michael J. *The Way of the Shaman*. San Francisco: Harper & Row, 1990.

Hill, Julia Butterfly. *The Legacy of Luna: The Story of a Tree, a Woman, and the Struggle to Save the Redwoods*. San Francisco: HarperSanFrancisco, 2001.

Jacobs, Alan. *The Principal Upanishads: The Essential Philosophical Foundation of Hinduism*. London: Watkins, 2007.

Kornfield, Jack. *A Path with Heart: A Guide Through the Perils and Promises of Spiritual Life*. New York: Bantam, 1993.

Mankiller, Wilma Pearl. *Every Day Is a Good Day: Reflections by Contemporary Indigenous Women*. Golden, Colo.: Fulcrum Publishing, 2011.

Moss, Richard M. *The Mandala of Being: Discovering the Power of Awareness*. Novato, Calif.: New World Library, 2007.

Peace Pilgrim. *Peace Pilgrim: Her Life and Work in Her Own Words*. Santa Fe, New Mexico: Ocean Tree Books, 1991.

Rain, Mary Summer. *Earthway*. New York: Pocket Books, 1990.

Rosenberg, Marshall B. *Nonviolent Communication: A Language of Life: Create Your Life, Your Relationships, and Your World in*

Harmony with Your Values. Encinitas, Calif.: PuddleDancer Press, 2003.

Ruiz, Miguel, and Janet Mills. *The Four Agreements Companion Book: Using the Four Agreements to Master the Dream of Your Life.* San Rafael, Calif.: Amber-Allen Publishing, 2000.

Smith, Huston. *The Illustrated World's Religions: A Guide to Our Wisdom Traditions.* San Francisco: HarperSanFrancisco, 1995.

Starhawk. *The Spiral Dance: A Rebirth of the Ancient Religion of the Great Goddess.* San Francisco: HarperSanFrancisco, 1999.

Stein, Diane. *Essential Reiki: A Complete Guide to an Ancient Healing Art.* Berkeley, Calif.: Crossing Press, 1995.

Tenzin-Dolma, Lisa. *Natural Mandalas: 30 New Meditations to Help You Find Peace and Awareness in the Beauty of Nature.* London: Duncan Baird Publishers, 2006.

Tolle, Eckhart. *Stillness Speaks.* Novato, Calif.: New World Library, 2003.

Trungpa, Chögyam, and Carolyn Rose Gimian. *Shambhala: The Sacred Path of the Warrior.* New York: Bantam, 1986.

Tzu, Lao, and Stephen Mitchell. *Tao Te Ching: An Illustrated Journey.* New York: HarperCollins, 1999.

Weed, Susun S. *Healing Wise* (Wise Woman Herbal series). Woodstock, New York: Ash Tree Publishing, 1989.

Wolff, Robert. *Original Wisdom: Stories of an Ancient Way of Knowing.* Rochester, Vermont: Inner Traditions, 2001.

ABOUT THE AUTHOR

Diana J. Ensign, JD, has explored Buddhist meditation, shamanism, Hinduism, Goddess rituals, Unitarian Universalism, Science of Mind, Twelve Step programs, and American Indian spiritual traditions. She has participated in Wisdom Circles and a Vision Quest. She is certified in Reiki III and practices T'ai Chi, Qigong, and yoga. With community support, she constructed a permanent outdoor labyrinth. She has also taken a nonviolent communication workshop and dream workshop. Diana is the recipient of an Arts in Indiana Grant for a project that featured veteran interviews and a 'Spirit and Place' public program, "Voices of Hope: Veteran Stories of Faith & Healing" (broadcast by Public Access Indianapolis).

Diana was born in Florida, grew up in Michigan, and graduated from the University of Michigan, Ann Arbor, (BA in English) and Wayne State University Law School, Detroit, (JD). She lives in Indiana with her husband and two daughters. She enjoys sunshine and hikes. Nature is her favorite wisdom source.

ACKNOWLEDGMENTS

I would like to thank the following people who gave their time, thoughts, and energy to birthing this book: Linda Neese (encouragement); Don Miller (Haiti outreach connections); Diane Loupe (professional edits); Gayle Thundar (manuscript read); Judy Wolf (professional proofreading and edits); Kate Oberreich (cover layout); Goddess Circle Group and Friends of Awakening sangha (support and love); family, friends, and veterans (for sharing stories); Robert E. Finnegan (for the gift of his gold retirement pen that reminds me of my path as a writer); Gloria Finnegan and Cindy Finnegan (for always being there in times of need); Dave, Indigo, and Emmeline (for abundant love and support of my dream).

I also extend gratitude to Bear Heart and Molly Larkin for permission to quote from, *The Wind Is My Mother*. While Bear Heart is no longer physically here, his Spirit remains strong.

For my author website, book cover photo, and author photo I am especially grateful to Marg Herder (www.circlewebworks.com). **Author Website: dianaensign.com**. Thanks also to everyone at Balboa Press publishing.

Special Thanks to Spirit and Trees

A percentage of this book's profits will go to the Lambi Fund of Haiti (working on reforestation in Haiti, along with sustainable development, environment, and women and girls' health, nutrition, and education).

"According to the UN, Haiti is the most severely degraded country in the Western Hemisphere—once plush mountainsides are now barren and devoid of trees as desertification kicks in. This has not always been the case though—as recently as fifty years ago, Haiti's forests were thriving and trees covered 60 percent of the country. **Today, less than one percent of Haiti remains forested.**" For more information, visit: www.lambifund.org

By purchasing this book, you make a difference.

Donations

If you would like to purchase this book in bulk as a charitable donation to Veterans Affairs centers; shelters, hospitals, prisons; or other nonprofit organizations, please contact the author at: www. dianaensign.com.

18048353R00117

Printed in Great Britain
by Amazon